This Book To
Belongs To
Patrick J. Hope
1/6/28

Given to Helen 2/26/75

# LIVING WATER

# LIVING WATER

PHOTOGRAPHS *Ernest Braun* – WORDS *David Cavagnaro*

AMERICAN WEST PUBLISHING COMPANY

PALO ALTO – CALIFORNIA

Passages from the following books have been reprinted by permission:

*The Firmament of Time* by Loren Eiseley (copyright 1960 by Loren Eiseley and The Trustees of the University of Pennsylvania, reprinted by permission of Atheneum Publishers, New York).

*The Flowering Earth* by Donald C. Peattie (copyright 1939 by Donald Culross Peattie, reprinted by permission of Noel R. Peattie, James Brown Assoc., Inc. (agent), New York).

*Galapagos—The Flow of Wildness* by Eliot Porter, foreword by Kenneth Brower (San Francisco: Sierra Club Books, 1968).

*The Immense Journey* by Loren Eiseley (New York: Random House, Inc., 1946).

*My First Summer in the Sierra* by John Muir (Boston: Houghton Mifflin Co., 1911).

*The Unexpected Universe* by Loren Eiseley (copyright 1964, 1968, 1969 by Loren Eiseley; reprinted by permission of Harcourt, Brace, Jovanovich, Inc., New York).

*The Web of Life* by John Storer (New York: Devin Adair Co., 1953).

*Western Star* by Stephen Vincent Benet (New York: Holt, Rinehart, and Winston, Inc., copyright 1943 by Rosemary Carr Benet; reprinted by permission of Brandt and Brandt).

*The Yosemite* by John Muir (New York: Doubleday and Co., Inc., 1962; reprinted by permission of Appleton-Century-Crofts).

Fifth Printing, July 1973.

Library of Congress Card Number 75-142443

ISBN 0-910118-20-5

# CONTENTS

# ABOUT THIS BOOK

The high peaks of a great mountain range lie tantalizingly close to our homes in the wooded hills of suburbia. Between these hills and the first slope of the range, a great agricultural valley extends as the only dividing feature of geography. On the one side, we lead our busy lives as photographer and teacher, caught up in the peculiar human pattern of survival. On the other, inhabitants of the vast mountain wilderness—pines and marmots, larkspurs, frogs, and a marvelous variety of other organisms—strive along an ancient path, living, dying, and perpetuating their kind in their own various ways. Between the two—between man and the rest of nature—lies a distance far wider than the great valley.

Even so, both of us, and many others who look toward rugged peaks and gentle alpine meadows, attempt to bridge this larger distance when we cross the valley at dawn and head for the mountains. We have hiked the back country separately and together, exploring, discovering, learning along the way. LIVING WATER is the story of many things we have seen and experiences we have shared—a story of life and water flowing, pulsing with the various rhythms of days, seasons, even centuries. Beyond this, what we say in words and pictures is a statement of how we view the delicate living fabric which envelops our globe, and how we view ourselves as human beings.

Like many others among our species, we are driven to escape from the walls, the asphalt, the smog, to places where our fellow earth-inhabitants still live more or less unharmed by man. There is no way to describe the joyous and peaceful feelings we receive from the natural world. We find a mysterious quality in the perfection of growth and the harmony of many creatures living together in balance, and we share a desire to move in close, to lie in the grass or stare into a stream where these processes can be seen in intimate detail.

We wonder also about ourselves as relative newcomers on earth. Man is only one of the many families of living things, no more deserving or important than any of the others except in his own eyes. In view of the devastating impact he has had on the ecosphere in so few years, nature may consider him an experiment as yet unproved. This unsettled question, also, has drawn us to the mountains.

We have come to a similar way of seeing because the wilderness has been our common ground. We have learned from it that though the earth speaks clearly it often speaks softly. The impressions come to all of our senses, and to some, perhaps, that we don't even realize we possess. We have learned that one must move quietly in the mountains with all doors open, and we must not be in a hurry.

This book evolved as freely as the river itself flows. A book was not planned in the beginning, but from the time the first pictures were taken about four years ago, through all the stages of writing, layout, and printing, the elements have fallen in place easily and naturally. Throughout the process, we have held firmly to the idea that subjective artistic expression and objective scientific fact are compatible.

LIVING WATER follows the stream, any stream, from timberline to the sea. The characters of the story are simply the peaks and meadows and living things we have encountered along the way. The principles of nature which they illustrate are universal. We speak of our own personal experiences, but they are available in similar kind to anyone who is willing to listen to the water of life flowing.

# IN THE BEGINNING

*these four—earth, air, fire, and water—formed the vital partnership from which life was born.*

The storm tide was running and the surf was high. Huge, frothing breakers boomed in against the rocky shore, splashing, tearing, receding, coming on again as if they were angry that the cliffs should dare to stand in their way. The sky was turbulent, the wind strong; nothing stirred save the waves, the rain, a thousand beach things blowing, and I, one lone creature exposed where the storm could find me.

I had the beach nearly to myself. The gulls had moved inland, waiting out the storm in the lee of coastal hills, and the sand crabs were deeply buried. Members of my own race were hiding, too, protected within the warm folds of technology, for people tend to stay in during days like this and keep the heaters going.

But many forms of life could not escape, those especially that were firmly rooted, such as succulents hugging the cliffs, facing straight into the salty wind; barnacles and mussels fastened tightly against the rush of breakers; and the dormant seaweeds, reduced to rubbery stalks and tough holdfasts which gripped the wave-battered rocks. I had these permanent residents to learn from, these that knew how to take a storm head on, and I held close in my own way to the land. I did not have to survive here, except for the moment, because my real

home was over the hill in the realm of man. I was out on the edge of things for the sheer joy of feeling small.

Life itself seemed diminished by the storm's powerful inland thrust. The mussels were lost in crashing spray and the cliff plants were veiled by blinding rain. The whole world seemed reduced to its basic elements: the earth, the bare spine of it jutting ragged and beaten into the waves; the air, swirling and storm-laden, carrying clouds inland toward the distant mountains; the water of the sea and driving rain; and the cloud-shrouded sun, whose energy drew the water up from the ocean reservoir and brought the storm into being.

Earth, air, fire, and water. It could almost have been a day from the time of creation itself. There was something in this storm that carried me back to the early beginnings billions of years ago, a time we can only guess about from the vaguest shards of remaining evidence. I clung to the rocks and let the storm engulf me with its ancient images.

The earth was a hot, molten sphere then, and the crust was thin and tenuous. Carbon dioxide, ammonia, and other gases bubbled to the surface as the molten rock solidified, remelted, and hardened again. At first most of

*Billions of years ago, as the molten earth cooled, water vapor condensed, fell, and began flowing. The first river was born.*

9

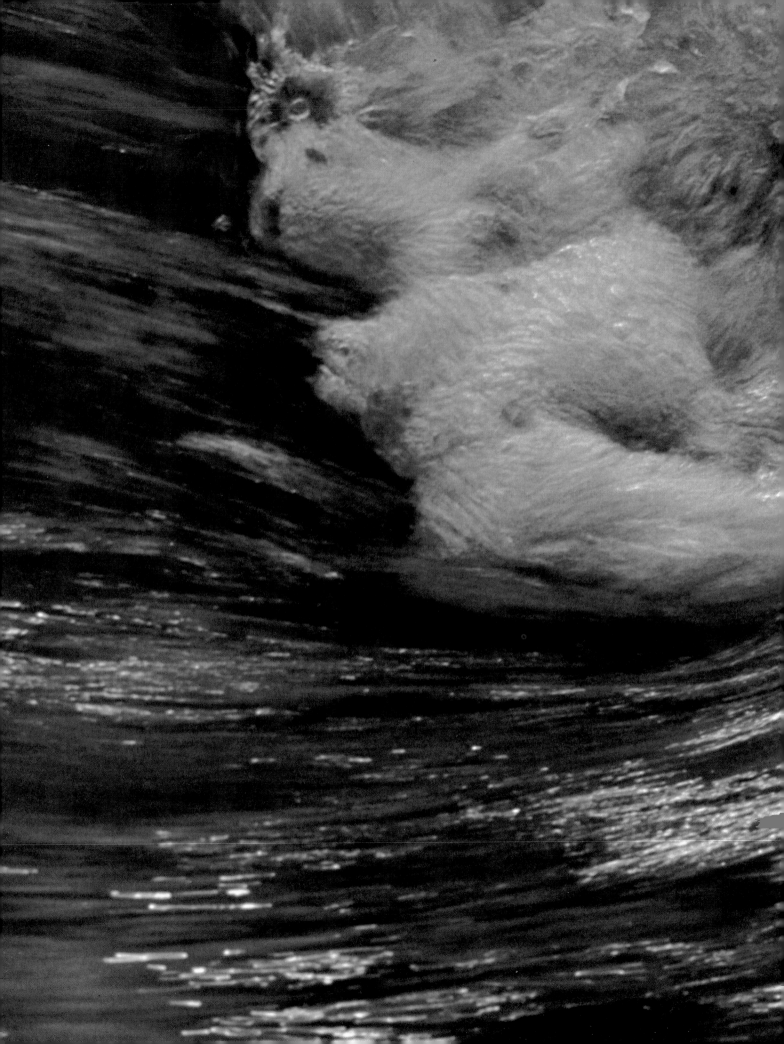

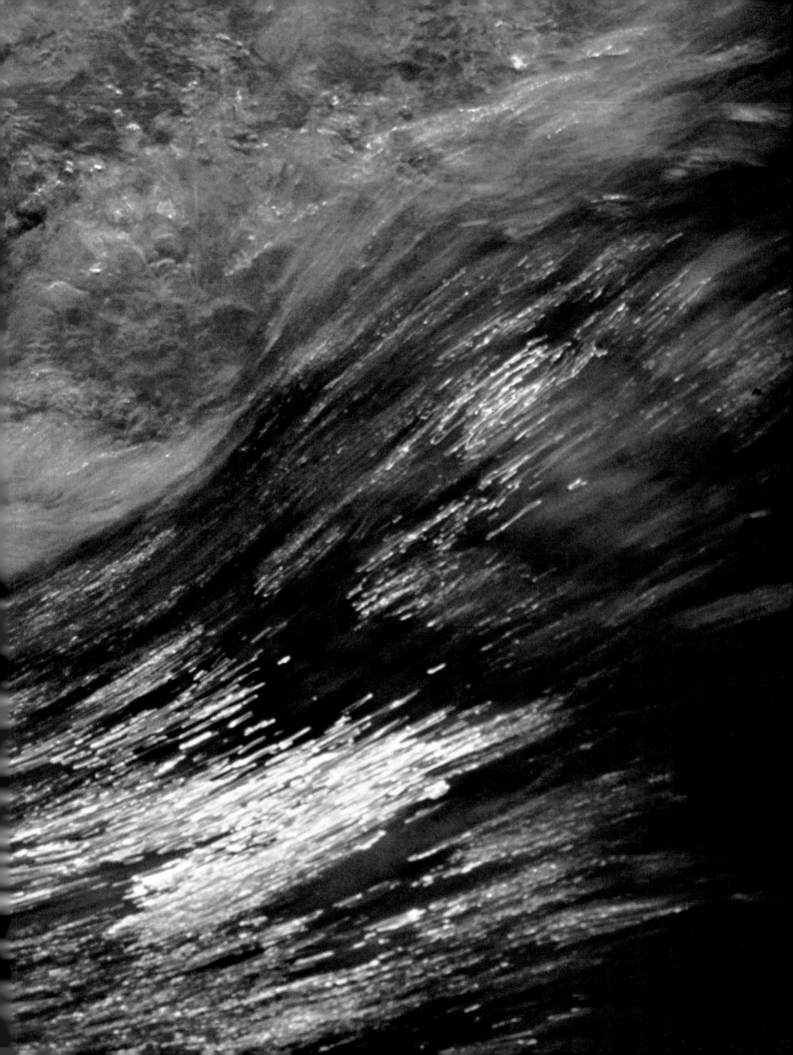

these vapors were lost to space, but as the earth cooled, the gases were held by gravity.

In this primordial atmosphere an important thing was happening which would change the face of the earth beyond our wildest expectations, had we only been judging the world from that end of time. For one of the new gases was water, and it filled the air as a vast cloud which enveloped the globe, casting a dark gloom upon all that was forming below.

For hundreds of thousands of years the great cloud thickened as violent eruptions hurled more water into the saturated air. Rain fell and was driven skyward as steam until somewhere, perhaps upon a young and jagged peak rising above the sweltering lowlands, the first fluid drop of water struck the land.

From then until now water has etched and carved, dissolved and scoured, just as I saw it working there among the seacliffs. The oceans have grown salty with minerals, their shallows full with sediments. Continents have been built and rebuilt, and the stuff of mountains has been carried away to the sea. Particle by particle, layer by layer, these muds and sands have accumulated, subsided, become compressed, folded, even remade into new kinds of rock, and thrust again into the clouds for another chance at becoming sand.

Sometime from two to three billion years ago, in the chemical ferment of warm, shallow seas, something new was happening even more incredible than the rise and fall of mountains. Ultraviolet rays from the sun had been building larger and more complex molecules from carbon dioxide and minerals dissolved from the air and the land. At last, but just when and how we do not know, these molecules became self-directive and self-perpetuating.

Minutely but steadily, living protoplasm altered in form and function, flowing through time and space, evolving, colonizing. Life has remained a vital partnership of earth, air, fire, and water, the elements from which it was born. From them have come the gull, the mussel, the seaweed, and man.

From then until now water has etched and carved, dissolved and scoured.
Particle by particle, layer by layer, the muds and sands of continents
have accumulated in shallow seas, subsided, became compressed, folded,
even remade into new kinds of rock, and thrust again into the clouds
for another chance at becoming sand.

What about man? I was a man, a teenager then, cast up on a storm-wracked beach with boulders and sand. I felt small, dwarfed by time and events about which I had only the vaguest understanding. I loved the sea and the storm, soaked and scared and cold as I was. I felt cut off from my own kind, and the waves had erased my trail. But I knew I would return by nightfall, over the hill to the place called home.

What would I be returning to, and what would I be leaving behind? I rose from my storm perch among the rocks and began searching along the trembling shore for some scrap that would tell me where I really belonged in the natural scheme of things.

Being young and unsure is a great thing, because doors are still open and there is room in one's soul for something as simple and unassuming as a walnut. I picked it up from the sand and felt its smooth, wave-worn shell. It was a black walnut, the wild kind I had seen growing along the creeks far inland, and I knew that it could only have come to this beach by way of the river.

I found it among heaps of logs piled against the cliffs, carried there also by the river and the sea. These were nature's castoffs, returning in time to the earth from which they came.

The signs of man were there, too, I soon discovered—a plastic bottle, a few tin cans, an old rubber sandal. Was this the best we could do? Were these our contributions to the earth? Was all that struggling of life up through the ages done for the sake of creating these trinkets? They had no worm burrows in them as the logs did, they wouldn't decay, they were set apart from the living.

It was then, with the storm surf flying, that I decided to follow the river. I felt more closely allied with the walnut than with the flotsam of my own race, and I asked myself why.

*Sometime between one and two billion years ago,*
*there arose on earth a new kind of chemistry—*
*self-perpetuating, evolving, colonizing—the chemistry of life.*

14

# AMONG THE PEAKS

*the naked rock arches high, lifting damp sea air*
*into the cold and jagged cradle of storms*

The river begins in little trickles among the mountaintops.

I feel close to the source in this high country, as though the origin of many things in the world were held here. The lofty range arches high, lifting damp sea air into the cold and jagged cradle of storms. The peaks are young and strong. They stand defiant, with teeth bared, resisting the ceaseless work of wind and water, unwittingly engaged in a contest their ancestors have always lost.

When the clouds lift, the sun rests heavy in the balance; the freeze teeters on its seasonal fulcrum and swings slowly toward thaw. Here, with the first liquid drops that flee the ice, the river finds its source.

Here, too, during the momentary pause of summer, the mountains contend for survival in another quarter. For among the sharp, silent corners of the crags lie the seeds of life, blown here by the wind. The hard spines of the range are the earth's very bones, and like whitened vertebrae cast as sand upon a distant beach, or a weathered, crumbling antler chewed by the packrat, these mountain bones are soon enough returned to the living.

Perhaps in that high mountain wind lies the true alpine genesis, birthplace of conflict and contradiction. For it is the same wind which one day plants the small, vibrant seed of a pine, waters it toward a frail but determined beginning, and the next day blasts the tiny seedling to shreds with granite sand. It is the same wind, thin and invigorating, that draws us to timberline and then drives us with sleet-swords into some frigid lee where a small fire flickers. This very wind tenderly delivers the snowflakes, then piles them deeper and deeper until together, as a mighty glacier, they sculpture the peaks and grind out valleys with an icy hand.

During an autumn visit to timberline one year I found the blueberries ripening and their leaves turning scarlet. A stillness hung over the high country like an invisible fog. I am a valley creature, I thought, come here as a foreigner, but something in the back of my mind nevertheless spoke of the advancing winter.

I leaned back against a gnarled root, the hidden, distant fear boiling up against my skull as the clouds swirled against a mountain far across an intervening canyon. It was a part of me beyond memory which knew about the glaciers.

*The hard spines of the range are the earth's*
*very bones. Among these sharp, silent crags lie*
*the seeds of life, blown here by the wind.*

An alpine wind carries winter
howling across high peaks.
Fire—a piece of the same minor
sun which gave man the edge
against the glaciers—holds
back the nightly vapors and
melts old ice-age fears.

With a shiver of ancient apprehension, I rose into the wind and hurried back to the warm haven of my campfire.

I huddled close beside the fire, thinking. The far clouds blazed briefly with the last light. Along a nearer ridge another cloud was creeping, dipping, playing with cliff edges. The cloud caught a small red glow and then snuffed it out in a mass of cold, gray vapors. The sun that brings the thaw had gone, and I was left alone with my little fire.

I remembered what I had read of man's beginnings, far away upon the warm savannas of another continent. Slowly, almost reluctantly it sometimes seems, the earth has yielded up a few clues from those early days, an occasional tooth or jaw fragment, scattered campsite middens, and some crudely worked pieces of stone. Our past lies as a fractured map with few locations marked and no routes between. We know only of some places where we have been, and must guess how and when we got there.

Our ancestors moved out across the land from their place of origin, evolving, adapting to new conditions they encountered along the way. They were food gatherers, taking from nature only what they needed.

They were, in those days of our dawn, more often the hunted than the hunter. But as these ancestral races penetrated northward across the Eurasian continent, they faced a new challenge which demanded more concentrated foods, hides for warmth, and the development of finer stone tools to obtain them. As they moved north, they became hunters, for a great sweeping cold and an abundance of large mammals were advancing southward to meet them. The first assault of the Pleistocene Ice Age had begun.

From 600,000 years ago to the present, vast glaciers have pushed down across the northern continents. Several times they have advanced and retreated, shrinking and swelling the seas, scouring the landscape, exterminating species and stimulating the evolution of new ones better adapted to harsh times. Even the tropical savannas, our early homeland, must have been chilled by tremendous ice sheets lurking beyond the mountains.

The early members of the family of man huddled in caves for shelter, their backs to the glaciers. While other species vanished or moved away, man lingered, for the same creative spark which fashioned the first stone tool had now, in this his time of need, kindled man's first use of fire.

The warmth I felt beside my campfire came perhaps as much from the ancient habit of fire tending as from the embers themselves. It was a warmth that held back the nightly vapors and melted the old ice-age fears. My fire was a piece of the same minor sun which gave man the edge against the onslaught of glaciers, the one tool with which he conquered the earth. Anthropologist Loren Eiseley has written of a cave in China where those early ashes rest, the record of cold nights 500,000 years ago when strange anthropoids sat by a fire, warming their hands as I warmed mine: "Fire contained, in that place of brutal darkness and leaping shadows, the crucible and the chemical retort, steam and industry. It contained the entire human future."

With spears chipped from stone man slaughtered the mammoths and cooked their flesh with fire. When the huge beasts were gone, he turned to other game, ripping and tearing at the resources of the earth for survival. We have never forgotten those glacial beginnings.

The flames spun around in a sudden vigorous draft. I noticed that snow had begun to fall. The most recent age of ice was pausing in its retreat to deliver us a snowclad winter.

*With one tool
—fire—
man conquered
the earth.*

The earth has seen many generations of mountains rise against the clouds and fall by the work of water. Mountain ranges are brief little anecdotes of earth history, and yet they are the whole world for plant and animal species whose existence they intrude upon. Perhaps nothing save submergence of land beneath the sea affects terrestrial life as profoundly as the emergence of mountains.

The sculptured, ice-polished rock I feel beneath my feet as I hike the high passes seems incredibly old, yet the granite spine of the range is young by geologic measure. The first signs of uplift began amid death rattles of giant dinosaurs. The rocks which were folded and faulted in that early range were more ancient still, for they were deposited as mud and sand in a shallow sea basin when the first scorpion-like arthropods were just scrambling hesitantly out of the ooze toward a dry shore. Today these rocks lie crumpled and discarded in the foothills far below the youthful crags.

The subsequent building of these and other recent mountains of the world destroyed old habitats, changed climates, and brought to a close the fantastic age of reptiles. By altering the flow of wind and water, and creating new zonations of temperature, these young ranges were shaping the evolution of innovative forms of life. Thus the mountains played their role in the proliferation of mammals, birds, and flowering plants.

While these momentous events were taking place on the slopes of our range and beyond, a great block of granite ten miles thick, millions of years in the making, was pushing up and cooling beneath its surface. The mountainous crest rose higher, creating, as time wore on, a great barrier which held back the sea-born clouds.

Beyond the peaks, in the rain shadow of the range, primitive horses and other grazing mammals roamed a dry plain while half way around the world, upon another grassland, the first man-like primates were exploring a new way of life. Strange mastodonts were evolving, diversifying, and among them were ancestors of the mammoths which would lure man across the Arctic Circle to North America during an ice age yet to come.

The advance and retreat of glaciers which shaped the destiny of man were only the most recent phrases etched in the history of the mountains. But like the last words spoken by a great orator, they have left the most profound impression. Alpine lakes, wide canyons, sheer cliffs, pounding cataracts, and jumbled moraines are the legacy of the Pleistocene iceflows.

Four times the ice advanced, wearing the old skin from mountainsides, exposing the massive core of granite which thrust the range skyward. After each glacial period plants recolonized the upper slopes, bringing timberline once again close to the sharp spine of the high country.

The winter now closing in upon the mountains, initiated by that first snow which swirled around my alpine camp, seemed by comparison with the glaciers a very small cold indeed, and yet every plant and animal knew of its coming. Marmots and pikas were safe in warm shelters beneath the talus; the beavers had already stocked their ponds with aspen branches; the deer and birds were foraging on lower slopes; delicate flowers were dormant as roots or seeds; and the twisted trees of timberline stood firm among the rocks, braced against another storm.

No living thing in this high place remembered the immense past written upon the peaks. But in their genes lay the hidden signals of recognition, the messages which told them what each must do, in its own way, to survive while the winter raged on.

*After glaciers, alpine winter seems a very small cold indeed.*

Ice spins lace on an alpine pond—or grinds
away the ancient rock of mountainsides.
Yet ice, from which living things flee, is
just the water of life in another form.

23

$S$now began to fall more heavily around my campfire that chill autumn night. It was my first visit with a timberline snowstorm, and the silent conversations one has with oneself during those moments of a first experience have a way of sticking tight to the fringes of the mind. I could almost smell the cold, if such is possible, and gusts of wind cut the flames into shattered, flailing little ribbons of orange.

There is something in a snowstorm that drives life back against the wall, and yet suddenly it occurred to me that the ice from which living things flee is just the water of life in another form. It was one of those commonplace facts, incredibly simple, that one learns from the pages of some musty textbook of physics but never truly knows until it falls out of the sky as a snowflake and melts on a warm knuckle. This is the kind of learning one never forgets.

Water molecules are simply hydrogen and oxygen atoms which were linked together in accordance with universal atomic laws as the molten earth began to cool. In that crucible of long ago bubbled the one chance for life on this planet.

These molecules of water respond now, as they did then, to the physical order of the universe. They react to each other, to neighboring molecules, and to changes in pressure and in temperature. Since their structure is unique, so too is their behavior. Life, death, and change occur in harmony with water's intrinsic properties.

From our human vantage, where everything somehow must have a purpose, it is difficult to imagine that nature could be driven by cause and effect alone. Nature is impassive and unsolicitous. Things happen in random fashion, not without cause but without purpose. In all the processes of living, water is simply there, indispensable, and life has made its adjustments accordingly. In that relationship lies the true magic of water.

The most singular quality of water is its occurrence in solid, liquid, and gaseous states within earth's normal range of temperature. Each, in some way, stands apart as special in its own realm. As a liquid, water has an exceedingly tenacious, skin-like surface tension. This attraction of water molecules to each other and to other substances enables water to rise up through the tiniest interstices of the soil by capillary action, riding as a thin film around every particle. Circulation of the vital fluids in plants and animals relies heavily on capillarity. Thus water is aided on its journey through narrow vessels from the roots to the outermost leaves of a giant tree.

Water is able to carry in solution nearly half the known elements without itself being altered. With carbon dioxide dissolved from the air, water forms a weak acid that etches minerals from rocks, as it did in forming the salty seas billions of years ago. Carrying minerals and gases in solution, water delivers to the cell of every living thing the substances needed for life. By the agency of water, all the complex activities of protoplasm are carried out. From all of these processes and the seething chemistry of life, this remarkable solvent emerges unchanged.

While liquid water is life's benefactor, ice is one of its principal antagonists. As water freezes, the molecules align themselves in an open latticework so that the solid is less dense and lighter than the liquid. When protoplasm freezes,

*Water's structure*
*is unique,*
*so too*
*its behavior.*

*To the ice piled broken on a timberline*
*lakeshore—to the awesome fact that ice floats—*
*life owes its continued survival on earth.*

the vital chemistry is disrupted and the cell walls burst under the pressure of expanding ice. Plants and animals have developed numerous ways of either avoiding or withstanding the rigors of freezing. Even so, the unexpected frost, severe blizzard, or advancing glacier takes its toll among the living.

Yet ironically this property of expansion places ice as perhaps the most fortunate anomaly in nature. To the ice piled broken against the shore of an alpine lake, or the iceberg floating south from beyond the Arctic Circle—to the awesome fact that ice floats—life owes its continued survival on earth. For if ice sank beyond the reach of the sun's warmth, the seas and lakes would long ago have frozen solid, and the great ice ages of the past would have persisted, possibly forever.

When ice melts, a tremendous amount of heat is absorbed, and another large sum of energy is required to move water from liquid to vapor. During thaw and evaporation, energy from the sun is taken up and efficiently stored by molecules of water. This unique association with heat creates conditions which have profoundly influenced the modification and distribution of living things.

Since most of the heat our planet receives from the sun falls upon the middle latitudes, convection currents are generated in the oceans and atmosphere as each is warmed unevenly. Aided by the earth's rotation, warm ocean currents from the tropics stream toward the poles, while frigid waters flow toward the equator. Similar patterns occur among the winds, distributing moisture and heat more evenly around the globe. The atmosphere and the sea are the earth's two thermostats, moderating climates and creating together all the phenomena of weather.

By regulating heat on a smaller scale, water creates microclimates to which living things have had to adapt as surely as they have adjusted to the larger climatic order. When water evaporates from a billion leaves, the forest air is cooled; when a lake stores heat on a sunny day, its shore is warmed at night. Among the stems and roots of a grass patch, the air is cool and moist, while overhead a hot wind rages; beneath the slow-melting snowpack winter still prevails, while above, on a rocky ledge, summer is advancing.

Water has these many peculiar qualities as a result of the unique union established billions of years ago between hydrogen and oxygen. Without the sophisticated tools of science, we cannot see the molecular structure of water; but as so often seems the case, there exists in nature a magnifying mirror in which we can perceive, by larger image, reflections of the minute.

For water this mirror is found in the delicate snowflake, a six-sided reflection of the angular bond which exists between two atoms of hydrogen and one of oxygen. Within this hexagonal theme, set according to atomic law, an infinite variety of form can exist. By the random accumulation of moisture from the air, snowflakes grow into patterns of magical beauty, not without cause but without purpose.

Life, too, is a kind of mirror for the structure and properties of water, but the reflections we see there are incredibly more complex than those we see in the growth of a snowflake. For life is a building, evolving, diversifying system, more perfectly balanced and beautifully con-

*Atmosphere and sea are the earth's two thermostats.*

ceived than man, for all his wisdom and sense of purpose, could possibly engineer. Water was simply there, in the beginning, indispensable, and life has made its adjustments accordingly.

The alpine wind carries winter howling across high peaks, driving everything alive into dormancy or hiding. Glacial lakes lie cold beneath a frozen rind. Rain turns to ice in rock cracks, pieces of mountains come crashing down, echoing, giving voice to the power of water. For life it is ebb time; for water, it is the season of ice and snow, sleet and hail. It is a time of violent fury and icy pauses. Low in the southern sky rides the sun, waiting.

Each morning of winter, in the spaces between storms, the sun rises against the mountains. Tentatively, the alpenglow kindles on the highest crag, and the sun begins exploring the intricate granite topography. But the shadows are still long, defying with a frigid cold the sun's penetration. Winter secrets lie hidden from the glare: a sculptured cascade of icicles, or the net-veined fabric of ice that grips the surface of a glacial pond. They catch reflections but not yet the heat of sunlight riding high along the granite walls.

Each day past winter solstice the sun fingers farther down the cliffs, probing, thawing, wrecking the ice-built magic of timberline. What the sun destroys a new storm builds again as warmth and cold wrangle among the peaks.

This coming and going of winter seems at times like a giant tug-of-war between fire and ice. Spring is winter's last stand against the advancing fires of summer, and timberline the final stronghold. High peaks and narrow clefts are a fortress for shadows where ice and cold huddle, waiting for fire's power to wane come autumn.

On cold spring nights in the mountains, I have often mused that night and day are simply minor versions of seasons or glacial ages. Lying with a view of the stars through a clear window of mountain air, I have at times even wondered if the entire universe might be an endless contest between fire and ice, with fire raging upon billions of celestial spheres and ice lurking somewhere in the void of space.

One night the mountains were especially cold. Ice needles started off early across the lake. chasing even the reflections of a retreating alpenglow. After a brief attempt to stoke the campfire, I retired to my sleeping bag beneath the stars. I pulled my head under, wrapped the fabric around my ears, and soon I was warm.

That set me to thinking. The fire was out, the sun was visiting in other lands, and yet I was warm where I lay protected, heated by the tiny fires of metabolism burning within every cell of my body. If the protoplasm in those living cells is mostly water, where was the tug-of-war between fire and ice? I realized that there is no battle at all, that fire and water, which seem intrinsically opposed, are really allied in a beautifully ordered balance, and that life is a highly refined manifestation of that alliance.

The next morning the sun pushed an inch farther into the icy shadows. Part of an old winter snowpack cracked away and tumbled into the lake, sending ripples across to the far shore. As little waves piled up against the bank, the entire sheet of nocturnal ice shattered, and a sound like the breaking of a thousand panes of glass echoed among the granite cliffs. In a

*Winter at timberline— a time of violent fury and icy pauses.*

*For life, winter is ebb time;*
*for water, it is the season*
*of ice and snow, sleet and hail.*
*Low in the southern sky rides*
*the sun, waiting.*

few moments the ice refroze, but within an hour the sun's rays were probing among the ice needles, returning them slowly to the lake from which they came.

Week by week with the approach of spring the sun gains upon the ice, with only occasional setbacks from late storms, much as a warmer climate has been advancing sporadically for twenty-five thousand years upon the heels of the last glacial period. The balance has many rhythms large and small, and sooner or later spring has its time. Wherever there is life, at the end of a marmot burrow or within the shell of a dormant seed, the little fires burn slowly, anticipating encouragement from the sun of springtime.

When water crosses that narrow threshold from solid to liquid, many hybernating metabolic fires stir, and the signal is given. A seed root bursts through its protective coat, probing for a foothold in the soil. A columbine buds green and tender from an old root in the talus, and the alpine willow, creeping prostrate through a mossy carpet, tests the air expectantly with swelling catkins.

Beneath the meltwater of a sloping seep, thousands of tiny bubbles of carbon dioxide announce the presence of life responding to the warmth of the sun. The plants are coming, they say, pushing up through old leaves where bacteria are renewing their efforts at decomposition. Ice has had its long winter nights and yields, reluctantly, to the lengthening days of spring.

The first shoots of spring launch themselves hopefully into the harsh world of timberline.

That initial step is a fateful one, especially for the sprouting seed whose single root represents the embryo's only chance for successful germination. Those seeds whose cellular time clocks were set too early risk death by the agency of a heavy freeze or late storm, while those which germinate too late may be crowded out or may mature and flower close against the rapid advance of winter. In either case, the ill-timed and unfit are sooner or later eliminated from the evolutionary mainstream, and each species is strengthened for survival in its particular timberline niche.

As the days lengthen, marmots and chipmunks emerge from hibernation, hungry and anxious to replenish their stores. Deer and birds migrate toward the high meadows from lower slopes, where signs of summer have already appeared. Insects wake from their winter sleep and begin worming, crawling, and chewing their way toward maturity.

As snowbanks recede, alpine plants spring into action, probing at the edges of the snow, almost chasing it into the shrinking shadows in their hurry to begin the season. The flow of life surges inexorably in every granite crevice and grassy hollow, each organism striving toward self-perpetuation, as the first living molecules more simply sought to duplicate themselves in warm seas of long ago.

In frigid glacial lakes and snow-melt ponds similar activity is soon in evidence. As the winter ice breaks up, frogs and mayflies lay their eggs in shallows among the reeds. Aquatic grasses reach for the water's surface; soon, as their leaves arch and bend over silver mirror-ponds, they will write their stories there in reflections like Chinese characters. I have gazed

*Fire and ice are allied in a beautifully ordered balance.*

for hours into those pools, wishing I could read the messages quivering there when the wind ripples are quiet.

I guess these tender water grasses speak mostly, in their happenstance ciphers, of the one quality which sets life apart from all the rest of chemistry, that peculiar self-directive nature locked within every cell. We call it, for lack of clearer understanding, the urge to live, the desire to reproduce. When we take apart this property of life, we find nothing more than a heap of atoms.

But from that heap an awesome order has been built, uniting atoms in molecules, cells in tissues, organs in organisms. Beyond that, organisms live together in communities, each playing its role in the intricate web of life.

The pond grasses grow indomitably each spring from the soft mud of glacial ponds. Spreading their leaves beneath the sun, they spend the short summer making food as only green plants can. The food they store in their tissues goes variously to their own roots for winter reserves, to scavenging tadpoles, larvae, and nymphs, and finally to bacteria, the great decomposers. Thus minerals that are left when the fibers of old leaf blades are gone are returned to the mud for reuse. From the death-like grip of another icebound winter, the delicate shoots will again unfold at the touch of a sunbeam, for that is the peculiar habit of every living green thing.

The alpine scene is constantly changing, and with it one's mood also changes. Our emotions seem more directly connected with the world here among the peaks than anywhere else. The shifting morning alpenglow, the glaring light of midday, the cloud shadow and billowing cumulus, the sudden thunderstorm come and go sometimes at a moment's notice. One is always alert at timberline, responding with quick breath and quivering senses to the rhythms of the day.

I'll willingly take whatever weather comes in the high country, but above all else I prefer the afternoon thunderstorms that build cloud upon cloud against the peaks. The beautiful white cumulus gather, dipping low among alpine lakes until the sky is closed off by a heavy gray curtain of mist.

The rumbling starts deep in the throat of the storm, swelling and dying and swelling again. When the full fury breaks overhead, it seems as though the world were being created all over again, so brilliant is the lightning, so loud is the thunder that rolls and crashes among the crags. A great deluge blasts at the granite; the ponds froth from the violent pelting, and the cliffs run with a thousand waterfalls.

The storm ends even more abruptly than it began. When I emerge from my shelter I expect to see a new mountain born of all that thunder-quaking, but there never is one. If anything, the peaks are just a little more diminished, imperceptibly eroded by the force of the downpour.

A flood of sunlight breaks through the clouds. The granite glistens, the air is clean and fresh, unburdened by the dusts and sprays and smogs of man which mantle the lowlands far below. The river born at timberline will soon enough cross those altered plains on its way to the sea, but for the present it trickles young and clean in a state of alpine innocence. I feel renewed and glad to be alive.

*When water melts, the signal is given.*

31

*Each day past winter solstice the sun fingers*
*farther down the cliffs, probing, thawing, wrecking*
*the ice-built magic of timberline.*

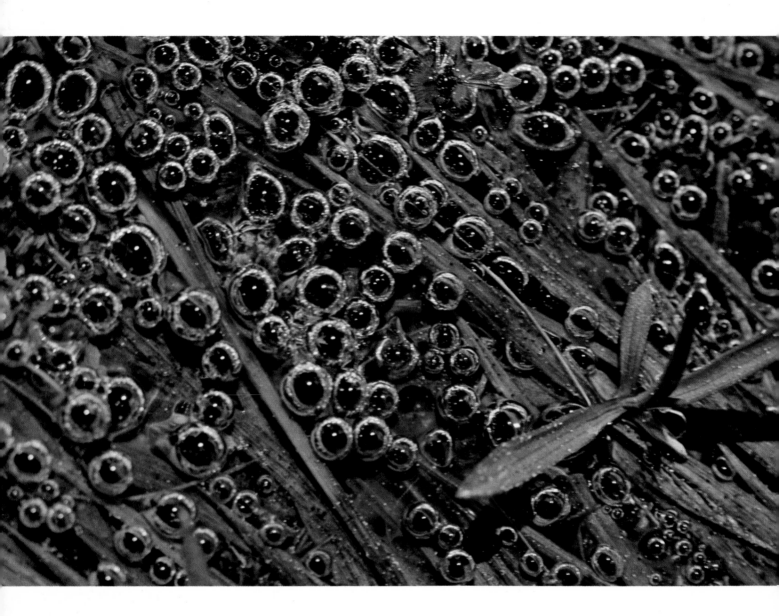

Beneath the meltwater thousands of tiny bubbles
announce the presence of life responding to the sun's warmth.
Bacteria renew their efforts at decomposition,
and the first shoots of spring launch themselves hopefully
into the harsh world of timberline.

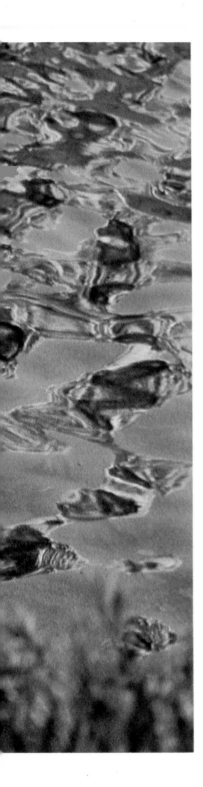

The alpine scene is constantly changing.
Shifting alpenglow, glaring sun, billowing cumulus,
and sudden thunderstorms come and go
sometimes at a moment's notice. One responds
with quick breath and quivering senses
to the rhythms of the day.

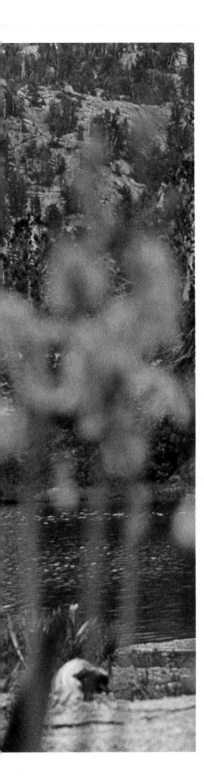

*Timberline summer*
*is a gentle*
*but busy time.*

Through still moments and thunderstorm moments, throughout all the days of this short, warm season, a feeling of exuberance pervades the high country.

I journey to the alpine meadows because something deep inside tells me I must share in this timberline feeling. The lofty range is my summertime sanctuary, a place to live outdoors with friends among friendly mountains. We shed most of our civilized trappings and camp beneath the stars, a few of us together, close beside a warm evening fire. I suppose we try, each in his own way, to return along those glacier-carved pathways toward our ancient beginnings. But there is no going back; the doors of time have closed behind us. This place belongs to other forms of life—the shooting star, the marmot, and the twisted pine. We are visitors only, and we come when the sun is high.

Maybe we eat a trout or two, and a few wild onions, but our lifeline extends to another place in another time. We come from valleys and cities, and the time is now. The wilderness is older than we, much older, and contains a wisdom which we must return here to find.

*Man is only one form of life among many others*
*which have already claimed the wilderness.*
*Though he may have the power to assume dominion*
*over them, he ought not cultivate the will.*

One morning, perhaps two thousand years ago, a chipmunk rose early and emerged from his burrow to search for food. Summer was waning in his small piece of high country, and little time remained for assembling his winter stores. If he was to survive the long, cold season ahead, he would have to spend the next weeks fattening up, and he started off upon his errand.

The pines were shedding their seeds, and the little squirrel scurried about beneath the ancient trees, scratching through heaps of needles, searching for his share of the rich, oily nuts. It was a good year for pine nuts, and he found many. He ate until he could hold no more, then filled his cheek pouches and began looking for convenient places to cache the extras.

He buried clusters of nuts in many locations, and during the following weeks, when most of the seeds beneath the trees had been found by neighboring squirrels and other animals engaged in the same task, he excavated for his hidden stores and feasted on them. By then the leaves of mountain blueberries were turning, and the nights were especially frosty. The first snow had fallen and melted; the little nut-gatherer was safely sleeping in his warm nest burrow. His heartbeat slowed, and his fatty tissues began yielding, in small amounts for the slow metabolism of hibernation, the energy stored from the pine nut harvest.

During his food-gathering frenzy, however, the chipmunk had hidden more nut caches than he was able to find. In a narrow crack between two gigantic slabs of granite, three pine seeds remained buried, protected beneath a thin layer of humus. They slept there through the winter in their own quiet state of dormancy.

The mountains looked then almost exactly as they do now. A few blocks of granite had not yet been added to the talus heaps, but otherwise the scene was scarcely different. Half way around the world, where men were keeping track of time, Christ had not yet been born.

When spring returned to timberline and snowbanks melted, the sun's warmth reached through the humus where the pine nuts waited. Water from the snow melt gradually percolated through their seed coats. The water awakened fires of life which had been burning the pine oils slowly through the winter, much more slowly even than the chipmunk consumed his fatty pine nut derivatives to stay alive.

When the chipmunk rose from his winter sleep he was hungry, but the three pine seeds had sprouted, and he passed them by. The tiny seedlings grew quickly in the warm spring sun. They sent down long taproots in response to a genetic directive hidden in their cells, and began growing needles like those dead ones about them on the humus, for pine begets pine in the manner of its kind.

As the young trees developed over the years, their genes directed the wood fibers in their limbs to strengthen against the rigors of wind and sleet. Eventually the first cones appeared upon the upper twigs, cones like those from which they had come as seeds. For two thousand years the three pines would share the granite crevice and the burdens of life at timberline. Their seeds in turn would feed many generations of squirrels. Some, scant few to be sure, would carry on the precious genetic code.

Starting from a time when the first conifers dominated the floras of the world, we might say that those genetic records were 200 million years in the making, for the codes of life are far more ancient than any single species that still lives upon the earth.

*The codes of life are more ancient than any single living thing.*

I must have been leaning against the root for an hour or so, but in my dreaming back twenty centuries to the hypothetical nut-gatherer, I had pretty much lost track of time. The sun was low, and the bark, the one strip of bark still alive after all those years of life, was in shadow on the lee side of the trunk. One sturdy limb still bore needles and even a few cones; the rest of the branches had been stripped long ago of their flesh and stood naked and silver in the late sun like a tangled heap of old antlers.

My hand went to the twisted root, still warm where I had been resting my back. The silver wood was smooth and polished; hard knuckles were exposed in relief where the fibers had resisted the relentless sandblasting gales of this high place. The root was not alive, and yet it still gripped the rock and held firm in the deep granite crevice.

I rose and studied the tree more carefully. I could see that the trunk was divided into three parts, as though perhaps the old pine had started as three separate seedlings, which eventually fused and became one. In one place the roots had outgrown their narrow crack and bulged over the granite; in another, they had been stronger or the rock weaker, for a large chunk of granite had been cracked off and forced free.

One set of branches glowed the color of rust in the setting sun, and when I climbed into the cradle of limbs, I could easily detect an ancient lightning strike, for even after years of sandblasting, a few streaks of charcoal remained. What monstrous storms, what spectral events this battered old tree had witnessed, no man would ever know beyond what he could guess among the scars.

If I had been able to see inside that gnarled and ancient thing, if I had been lucky enough to browse along a core sample extracted from its heartwood, I would know its story much more intimately, for in the growth rings would be written the history of its life.

The little chipmunk would remain forever among the guesses; he came too early to leave a mark. But most other important events would be recorded somewhere amid those thin annual rings. There would be, in this woody journal, records of heavy winters and dry years, perhaps of decades that were warmer or colder than others. There would be deep scars left by lightning and small tunnels inscribed by beetles. An unusually severe sleet storm might have added its signature where the trunk bent low and crumpled slightly beneath the weight of ice. We could read, too, when the various branches died, were snapped off, and their stubs engulfed by the advancing, healing bark.

Before I left the old pine on its windswept ridge that summer evening, I stood for a while watching the last sunlight blaze along timberline, creeping up the jagged slopes until it passed the final line of stunted trees. They are the mountain scribes, I thought, manning the last outpost. In their wood-fiber diaries lie the permanent records of many fierce winters, for though the chipmunk can hide and the columbine can die back to a protected root, these rugged conifers have no place to turn but straight into the wind.

This awesome, forbidding place belongs to them more than to any other living thing. I am only a visitor here, I realized as the sun set and the chill of night advanced over timberline. Man's principal attribute as a guest of the scribes, I thought, is his ability to read their version of history.

*Alpine trees are mountain scribes manning the last outpost.*

43

*Timberline pines stand like tangled heaps of weathered antlers. What monstrous storms, what spectral events these battered old trees have witnessed, no man will ever know beyond what he can guess among the scars.*

Beyond timberline, where peaks and clouds clash and blowing sand grains chip away relentlessly at the granite spine of the range, we find the extremities of life, thin extensions of the living film that surges up the slopes, defying the rock and storm.

A few spiders lurk among the crevices, preying upon insects blown here beyond their element. And lichens hug the cliff faces—tough, crusty little patches that look more like outgrowths of rock than products of the plant kingdom. From the moment when the spore of a lichen takes hold on a windswept shoulder of granite, the mountains can never again be the same.

Were the contest left solely to wind and water, peaks would be split and broken by ice, their angular faces ground smooth by glaciers, their stony chips rounded by rivers, pounded from boulder to gravel, from pebble to sand, all in the wink of an eye by earth time. And this would be all.

But water in its living forms, combined in many kinds of complex molecules, has gained much in experience since the first great rains dragged barren crags, broken and dissolved, toward the sea. When plants first left those ancient shallows, laden as they were with the ooze and salts of mountains, they took with them in their living protoplasm a small part of the sea. For half a billion years plants have been experimenting upon the land. Many have marched against hostile slopes, the source from which they came as water and minerals in times long ago. But the water and nutrients swept past them in muddy torrents. How, then, could they hold back a little parcel of the life-giving fluid to replenish their thirsty proto-

plasm? Every land plant that ever lived has had to answer that challenge.

From persistent experimentation has come that first lichen colonist of the high granite. Many other kinds of plants have evolved to follow the lichen's initial pioneering, each altering the rock a little more, retaining the grains of sand, conserving water, slowing the mad rush of erosion, yet changing the land in the subtle ways that solely belong to life. For only by the hand of the living does sand become soil. At the insistence of life, the peaks exchange their primordial innocence, particle by particle, for the newer and more refined experience of living things.

The process of soil formation begins with rock weathered by wind and water. The crumbled components of timberline granite collect in cracks and small depressions. There, by the root and needle of the ancient pine, or the decaying stems of alpine grasses, the amazing amalgam called soil is formed.

The key figures in this process are the scavengers and decomposers. A host of tiny insects and other arthropods chew away at the plant wastes, reducing the accumulating organic material to humus. Meanwhile the decomposers are at work digesting these last plant remains, slowly breaking down cellulose and other complex organic materials and releasing back into the substrate the basic nutrients needed for plant growth.

Bacteria and fungi play the vital role of returning the productions of life to the source from which they came. These decomposers complete the beautifully balanced and essential cycle of re-use; without them there would be no such thing on our planet as soil.

*Only by the hand of the living does sand become soil.*

46

The decaying humus, interwoven roots, and underlying weathered rock constitute a stable fabric which retains water and minerals, protects the rock from rapid erosion, and provides plants with the substances needed for growth. Soil is like a living tissue which pulses with billions of microscopic units of life, a fragile skin which gradually covers the earth's bones. Under the best conditions, five hundred years may be consumed in producing one inch of soil; and at timberline, where the climate is cold and the decomposers are slowed in their work, much more time may be needed. Yet the slightest disturbance—a small landslide or a shift in the course of a stream—may wipe out in a few hours the work of a thousand years.

But most of the soil holds, bound together by a meshwork of roots, protected from the rain by a tangle of growing plants or a mat of humus. Vital nutrients are only slowly lost through the forces of erosion, and they are replaced as the parent rock gradually dissolves.

Ever since the scouring of the last glaciers, patches of soil have been accumulating, expanding, filling the crevices and protected hollows of timberline. In these precious pockets, rich with the materials of life, grow the incredibly beautiful gardens of alpine spring.

When the Cassiope blooms, the mountains seem to sing with laughter. The little heather-bells glint white and waxen in the sun, inviting bumblebees for a meal. There is a burst of energy, a surge of joy, until it appears to the human visitor that the whole range is warm and radiant.

It may only seem so to us because we view the world from that peculiar place of being human and can share with some sentimentality in the exuberance of beginning a new season. We browse through a hundred little hanging gardens which bloom here among the crags, and we revel in the happiness of growth and the fulfillment of blossoming as though under the influence of some contagion.

Perhaps the feeling is catching because we can identify with these delicate alpine flowers more than we can with the old, gnarled pines, for, after all, the flowers are out beneath the summer sun as we are, when the grass is parched and brown in the lowlands and winter is only a fearful memory. The sweet-scented lupine, scarlet paint brush, shooting star, columbine, gentian, and mountain heather seem like compatriots which sneak in quickly between a late spring thaw and early autumn storms. Perhaps the contagion comes from the fact that they are, as we are, a part of the alpine contrast.

But there is more to be learned among the warm, scented gardens of timberline, for every flower and grass and moss growing here is firmly rooted in an ancient soil which they and their ancestors helped to create. They have summer in their leaves and flowers but winter in their roots and seeds, because they must stay with the soil, to which they are forever linked, and with the water of melting snow, which courses through their veins.

When the alpine gardens bloom, they bloom from the richness of rock and from all that living things have done with that rock through centuries of growing and dying. In the splendid tapestries of these gardens the beauty of death as well as the beauty of life finds expression.

*Bacteria and fungi complete the essential cycle of re-use.*

*When the Cassiope blooms, it blooms from the richness of rock
and from all that living things have done with that rock through many
centuries of growing and dying. In the gardens of alpine spring
the beauty of death as well as the beauty of life finds expression.*

For some still puzzling reason many of us return year after year to timberline. We are more than just stray wanderers, for all those who journey on foot or horseback to these hidden meadows among the clouds seem to come as on a pilgrimage. It is as though we are each hunting along the high cliffs, in the white-billowed cumulus, among the weather-worn pines or the water-grass reflections, sifting for something among all the objects and incidents of timberline. Why else would we trouble ourselves to take this alpine leave from the place we now call home?

Perhaps we just need a new scene, a change from a way of life that soon enough becomes routine. Maybe we need to relax, let go, loosen our grip on our daily accounts. Some of us may come to study botany, watch the behavior of the pika, or trace the movement of vanished glaciers. Or might it be that we are probing through these mountain heaps for some missing connection that would link us forever to this wild place; that would, as John Muir said of other things in nature, hitch us also to everything else in the universe?

As long as there have been words to speak and glyphs or alphabets to write, men have struggled to understand and define their place in the natural order. Ancient cave paintings tell their version; Japanese prints and the art forms of a thousand other peoples past and present tell theirs. Hundreds of faiths and thousands of temples have been erected as answers in the darkness of the unknown. Thoreau, Darwin, Eiseley, and a whole library full of other naturalists have lived among the bones of the past or the creatures of the present and have written of what they learned there. Muir has strived for his definition in the wilderness of mountains, and I suppose that in this little journey with water I'm adding my own cave paintings to the multitude.

In all this time man has not yet defined his place and his role to his own satisfaction. At least there certainly remains much difference of opinion! It's just as well, perhaps, because the wilderness seems the brighter, as a cave, with a question always burning at the far end. Maybe that uncertain glow in the far rooms of the mind is what draws us to this wild, wind-swept corner of timberline, for here we reach the source of the river, the origin of many questions, and perhaps even some answers.

Thoreau implored, "Keep your accounts on your thumbnail," and in his rustic, wild life he sought what answers concerning man and nature this policy would bring him. I must admit with some regret that my thumbnail needs a good deal of trimming, but I do embark upon the task when I plan a hike to timberline.

Sleeping bag, tarp shelter, boots, matches, a pot or two, Sierra cup, down jacket, rope, poncho, and flashlight are collected in a comfortable, lightweight backpack. Dehydrated food, some sticks of jerky, a bag of coffee and a few packages of Lifesavers are added, and a camera for recording memories. Forty pounds for a week and the clothes on my back. I imagine Thoreau would have scoffed at such luxuries. The Indians, who followed the seasons with the deer and berries and acorns, simply wouldn't have known what to make of these trappings.

Nevertheless, by valley standards this mountain baggage seems light indeed, reduced to a sort of bare-bone economy. A week in the high country is a purge of certain civilized notions, and a month would be better. The idea that all food must come in cans and bottles, that we must live in a sort of cocoon where the air is

*The economy of living is a balanced plan for survival.*

50

always 70 degrees, that heat and transportation must be generated by an ancient legacy of fuels left over from a time that will never be repeated, that everything wild must be killed or tamed, that all the land must be owned and every foreigner is suspect—these and a hundred other old-habit ideas crumble at timberline, because in the alpine economy there is neither room nor time for such extravagance.

We can't return to the life of the Indian, for those doors, too, have closed behind us. But there may be something to be learned about ourselves from a short stint of timberline living. Nature itself is economical in this high, rugged place because every living thing must be, in order to survive. Time is short between the last snow of one winter and the first snow of the next; the pika must store his hay piles, the lupine must set seed. Even with all our extra baggage, life among the peaks is tough, and we soon learn what economy means.

On my own treks I have noticed how the timberline economy takes hold. My stews, it is true, come from fields and valleys far away, spiced maybe with a few wild onions gathered here. But the packaging is simple; no metal cans will rust here among the old pines, forever unretrievable. Because of my lifeline with agriculture, I fish the alpine lakes more for pleasure than for survival, and yet I am forced to realize that so frequent have been the visits of fishermen here that were the lakes not stocked from time to time, perhaps no fish could be found at all. And when I probe among the ancient pines for firewood, I soon remember that I and others who come here must not burn the precious wood faster than the death of limbs and the work of winter storms can provide it.

Transportation is of my own making, and it relies only on stew and trout and a handful of wild onions for fuel. I walk for days over granite that belongs more to the old glaciers than to anything alive. The government has said this land belongs to everyone, and that includes especially the pines, hemlocks, grasshoppers, and other permanent residents.

Nothing need be killed that isn't promptly eaten, and there is no reason to suspect the neighbors; the marmot and the mountain heather are friendly enough. Even the bear and rattlesnake of lower elevations strike, as a rule, only when provoked, much the same as people. Those folk who come to timberline generally come for a reason, to find the source perhaps, to live with the natural rhythms of the place, and their aggressions seem to atrophy for want of cause. I rapidly find it useless to view such people with suspicion.

*Alpine living is beautifully frugal and exacting.*

There are many alpine economies. The economy of living: warm, busy rhythms of the day, plants growing, caterpillars chewing, the morning cup of camp coffee, the cool drink of ice-melt water, the incredibly good food—just enough and no waste—and a long, searching hike among the crags. The frigid bite of nightfall, fire warmth, camp shelter, and pond plants frozen solid in a needled stitchwork of ice.

Each plant and each animal takes from its environment the water and the food it needs to live and returns to the land, sooner or later, its entire substance. The economy of living here, as anywhere, is a balanced plan for survival, an

*The morning cup of camp coffee,*
*a cool drink of ice-melt water,*
*the incredibly good food,*
*a long, searching hike among the crags,*
*the frigid bite of nightfall,*
*fire warmth and camp shelter—all*
*are contained in the balanced economy*
*of alpine living.*

eternal cycle of life, death, and re-use, beautifully frugal and exacting. The times are just tougher here, and the economy seems a bit more stringent.

There is also the conservation of energy and motion. It is perhaps more evident here than in milder climates that the energy needed for living, that precious energy which comes from the sun, must be preserved and used to the best advantage. The sedge must store in its roots the food its leaves have made with the help of the summer sun; the chipmunk must fatten up on pine nuts to survive the winter. We learn, as the animals have learned, that we must not expend more energy in our timberline pursuits than our food supply can replenish.

Even the water, in its own passive way, seems economical in its motions. It responds to the rhythms of day and night, thawing, freezing, and thawing again, running drop by drop, a million drops together toward the sea. The little streams flow submissively, governed only by gravity and topography, mumbling, gurgling, skipping, sliding—yet making not one wasted motion, following always the path of least resistance.

Some of the water runs straight away to the ocean. Some percolates slowly through the soil, penetrates hidden membranes in many dark, subterranean passageways, and enters the peculiar chemistry of life, only to be transpired again into the air. There the vapors join the clouds and fall again in a summer thundershower, or blow on beyond the range to etch their phrases upon some other landmark.

What wondrous stories a water molecule could tell, of wild peaks visited on stormy nights, of quiet rivulets and raging rivers traveled, of peaceful fogs and sun-colored clouds,

*Water, like life, exhibits a basic natural economy.*

of glaciers and ocean currents, of fragile snowflakes and crisp little frost crystals, and of the seething protoplasmic retorts of living cells—a zillion places visited since the earth's beginning. If only the water could speak our language, but instead we must read of its work among the rocks it etches and tumbles, and among the living organisms it helps to fashion.

At the source of the river and all along its course, we find that water, like life, responds to a basic natural economy. No wound it inflicts, no matter how severe, leaves a scar which cannot be healed eventually. No mountain range is worn away that cannot be rebuilt, no plants are torn from the ground that cannot be re-sown, no rain falls to the earth that cannot be evaporated again in a moment or a million years. The water cycle is impartial, efficient, and splendidly economical.

At timberline, there exists another important economy, that of time. The season of warmth is short, and everything alive must know it or die. Many times I have seen mountain heather blossoms frosted with a late snow powder, or flowers of alpine summer bruised and crumpled by a severe, unseasonal freeze. Life at timberline is a parenthetical affair, pinched and bracketed at its spring and autumn extremities, until in some places, beneath snowbanks left over from a heavy winter, warmth never comes at all, and the living roots and seeds must wait for another chance at summer.

One senses a tremendous urgency among alpine organisms, for each seems in its own way to be in a hurry, the more so as the season advances. No one wants to be caught short, least of all we who have made no provisions for winter. An early snow sends our nerves tingling and awakens those old Ice Age fears which must be lurking somewhere in our gene fabric.

The frantic hubbub of alpine summer is only one hand, however, on nature's timeclock. There are others which move faster and still others which move slower. Millions of years are required to build mountains, millennia to make soil. The eagle that soars upon mountain updrafts matures in three years, the lupine in a season, bacteria in a few hours. There are many timberline times, and each has its own economy.

There is something about emerging from our cocoons into the bright, clean air of wilderness that carries us back to the source, if only figuratively. There is something in cause-and-effect wilderness living—a directness, an immediacy, a balance—that awakens shapeless memories.

Somewhere back along the precarious course upon which our species has embarked, those memories were kindled, perhaps in the first fire our ancestors tamed, the first stone tool they chipped, or the first field they tilled. Those tarnished, age-worn memories remind us that once we, too, had an economical life style. We took from the land only what resources we needed and returned them in re-usable form. Our numbers were small, our requirements simple, and we lived in balance with the web of life.

But gradually our numbers and our abilities increased. We extended ourselves beyond the web and began exerting over the natural balance a power without precedent in the history of the earth. We began taking from the land more than we returned and altering the balance faster than it could be restored. Now, as our pace accelerates, we seem to find ourselves estranged from everything wild, embarked upon a frightening, often exciting, and increasingly lonely journey. We are now man apart, controlling some of the webstrings of life itself. The responsibility of this mission is more enormous than we may ever know.

Along the mountain stream the original economies still prevail. The web of life is still a web unbroken, with each organism hitched to every other, and to the land, the air, the water, and the sun, in a state of mutualism nearly two billion years in the making. Have we relinquished our place in this ancient system of balance? Have we taken our distance?

When we come to these mountains, we are only summer visitors. When the first snow clings beyond a day to the timberline pines, we beat a hasty retreat. But the same unsettled questions will draw us here again another year, that we may slowly understand what we have rejected, that we may learn what it is we have chosen to rule, that we may evaluate the wisdom of our course.

The stream flows on toward the sea, through another winter and another spring, among beautiful, expansive mountains, tumbling wild and clear from a source nearly untouched, as yet, by our peculiar, human dilemma. Maybe the mountains, the stream, and all the living things along its banks hold for us the answers we are seeking, ancient rules that the twisted pine, the chipmunk, and the columbine obey, that we ourselves understood long before there was ever need to question.

As the stream is born of a snowbank or passing cloud, in this one magic quality of wilderness we, too, find our source.

*Once man, too, lived in balance with the web of life.*

*Water responds to the rhythms of day and night, thawing, freezing,*
*and thawing again, making not one wasted motion, running*
*drop by drop, a million drops together toward the sea.*

The warm sun of midday and the icy chill of night, mild summers and
severe winters, all must be taken in stride by alpine plants
if they are to survive, for they are merely guests of the climate.

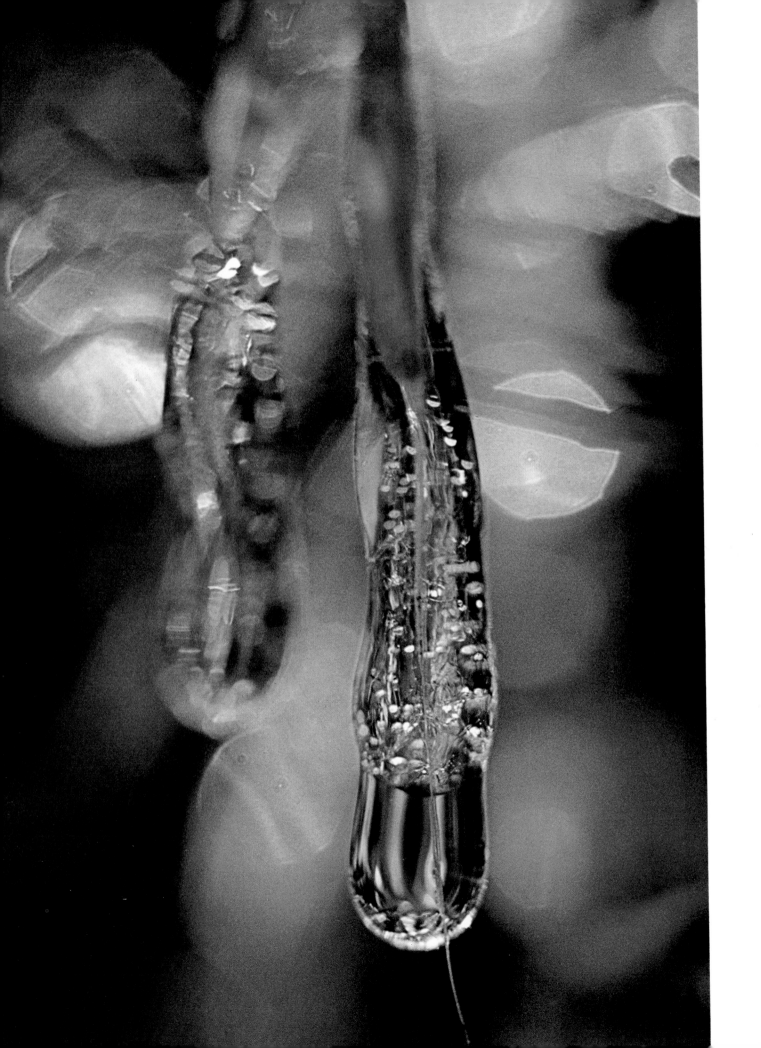

What wondrous stories a water molecule could tell, of wild peaks
visited on stormy nights, of quiet rivulets and raging rivers traveled,
of the seething protoplasmic retorts of living cells—a zillion
places visited since the earth's beginning.

Life at timberline is a parenthetical affair,
pinched and bracketed at its spring and autumn
extremities. One senses a tremendous urgency
among alpine organisms, for each seems in its own way
to be in a hurry, the more so as the season advances.

*When winter returns, water is held back again at the source,*
*in the ice-covered lakes and blizzard-glazed snowfields*
*of timberline, and in the vast carpet of snow which stretches*
*unbroken along the stream to the lower slopes of the range.*

# BESIDE THE STREAM
*growing things draw water from the noisy
flood to feed their silent chemistry*

The moment of enchantment was contained in a mountain forest during the dead of winter, for as a child I never knew snow. An Eskimo might find such magic in a tree, a midwesterner in the foam and spray of breakers dashing against the coast.

I had never before been on snowshoes. It must have been a remarkable sight; I felt as though I had eight legs and glue on the bottom of my feet. But in fits and starts I struck off toward an eerie cathedral of giant firs. Looking back over my monstrous trail, it occurred to me that the real abominable snowman might simply be a novice on snowshoes!

Once in the forest, the strange white world of winterland closed in around me. A fresh snow had fallen during the night, and the sky was still laden with heavy, menacing clouds. My heart soon pounded from the drag of inexperienced feet, until I could no longer hear the awesome silence of this strange new landscape. I felt alone and exuberant.

A tiny breeze drifted through the high limbs. Several large puffs of snow slid from the fir boughs and rained down with a powdery swish. I was looking for something familiar, something that would tell me for sure what I already knew, that I had been here before when the dogwoods were blooming and the spring sun was warm even in the forest. I saw it finally, a twisted old limb I had noticed the year before jutting from the trunk of an old fir. My god, how much snow is there here, I must have asked aloud. I remembered looking fifteen feet up at the lichen-covered snag, while now I was seeing eye to eye the peculiar knot that made a serpent's head of the limb's broken end.

A bit farther along I came upon a fox trail and followed his fresh tracks through the snow. Twice I found places where he had dug into a drift in search of food. In spite of numb fingers and toes, I could only think what a beautiful place this would be to spend the winter. The struggle to stay alive didn't for the moment cross my mind.

By the time I reached the stream, a soft snow had begun to fall. The world seemed geared in slow motion, as though time were running down and any moment the flakes would stop falling completely, to remain suspended in the grip of a permanent winter magic. Even the stream was running slowly. The water was being held back at the source, in the ice-covered lakes and blizzard-glazed snowfields of timberline, and in the vast carpet of snow which stretched unbroken along the stream to the lower slopes of the range.

The stream that I had known in the full fury of spring thaw, dashing, splashing, tearing at the boulders which dared to obstruct its course, this mountain stream that I had heard from a distance as it roared through the forest, was now quiet. Its substance was locked in the intricate needlework of a mammoth ice fabric, its energy measured in potential only. A small trickle managed to defy the icy hold of the snowpack, and it ran almost hesitantly among white, puff-covered rocks and beneath thick, laden snow bridges, which here and there obscured its flow completely.

It was a time for storing up, for replenishing reserves. Except for the howling blizzard and the sleetstorm, it was a quiet business.

Beneath the drifts, seeds and roots, saplings and rodents, eggs and pupae lay hidden, all reduced to their own state of dormancy yet insulated from the fatal stabs of winter. Above them, all around them, was the protective envelope of snow, an insulating matrix of air and ice, draped across the mountains in every direc-

*Winter is a time for storing up.*

tion farther than I and my snowshoes could walk in a month, at the rate I was going. The thought of it made my feet ache! I was standing above all these sleeping things, on top of a giant sponge, next season's reservoir, life blood of the forest itself and of the stream. By next summer this snow would be coursing through the veins of ground squirrels, the nectar glands of lupines, and the limbs of every fir in the forest. Some would have returned to the air, bound for a distant thunderstorm. And some would be pounding its way from stream to river, up the roots of a far-off valley cotton-wood, through a corn-farmer's irrigation ditch, out the end of a garden hose, or the nozzles of a carwash, or the siphon of a bay clam. But for the present, here it all was, clean and white —a giant store of water, and temperature its only dam.

The wind picked up and more snow slid from the fir branches. A swift gust of frigid air bit into my back and passed on through the forest. The tall firs swayed and answered the wind as only trees can answer. I replied with chattering teeth and began at that moment to appreciate what these forest giants must endure.

I wondered if they, too, had some way beyond our perception of remembering the glaciers which pushed them far beyond the northern latitudes and then, in their retreat, left great moraines for these trees of the north to re-colonize. In that winter snowstorm, mantled as they were in white, the firs seemed like refugees caught between a frozen northland and deserts to the south, between icebound peaks above them and dry foothills below. I thought of the groves I had seen on the tops of mountains in the Southwest, stranded there when the cold pulled back. A few degrees of warming in the local climate and they might dwindle away for want of snow and their seed-lings wither in the summer heat.

But here, nourished by winter snow, summer rain, and cool breezes, in a climate comparable to latitudes much farther north, the big forests thrived. I was standing upon one of the reasons for their healthy presence, the snowpack, and I realized that in one way or another water was dictating the survival and the distribution of these noble trees.

Snow and firs are inseparable winter part-ners, but the trees are not always treated kindly. When I returned to the mountains the follow-ing spring, I saw that severe blizzards had stripped the needles and in some cases even limbs from some exposed trees. It had been a hard winter. More snow had fallen in the mid-dle altitudes of the range than old-timers had seen in decades. When the pack finally melted, many saplings lay bent or broken from the weight. Some would gradually straighten, oth-ers would send out new main shoots. But a few would probably be left behind to perish in the shade as their more vigorous neighbors reached skyward.

That gloomy thought took on added signif-icance as the snowfall suddenly increased. Even with snowshoes I was sinking more deeply in the fresh powder, and I began to feel far less suited than the firs to a winter burial. The magic of the moment was one thing, but too much magic rapidly began to seem unhealthy. I left the stream in its icy slumber and staggered awkwardly back through the forest.

I felt incredibly pleased with my success in a new element as I rested in the cabin beside a warm fire, as though I had somehow managed to walk on water. In fact, I guess I had!

*Might the firs, too, remember the glaciers?*

Spring comes to each tiny stitch in the snow quilt as a single moment. Molecules in the ice lattice soak up energy from the sun until they break the close tie they may have held all winter with their neighbors. In that supreme moment, essential to all life, ice becomes liquid. It is the fluid instant.

Opening the stores is the first task of spring each year. Everything alive waits for the job to begin—willow leaves locked tightly inside their waxy bud scales, congregations of ladybird beetles hibernating in the lee of a fallen log, corn lily shoots poised and ready in the darkness of the buried meadow, deer browsing in foothill canyons where spring has already left its first marks. They all wait in unison for spring thaw, for sunlight to penetrate the white blanket of winter and give the signal.

Spring comes to each tiny stitch in the snow quilt as a single moment. Molecules in the ice lattice soak up energy from the sun, become more and more agitated, until they break the close tie they may have held all winter with their neighbors. In that supreme moment essential to all life, ice becomes liquid. It is the fluid instant.

For the plants and animals of the mountain slope, however, spring advances more hesitantly. A warm spell sends meltwater crashing downstream as though the thaw were in full swing. The snow line creeps back through the yellow pine forests and slows in the deeper drifts beneath the firs. The sweet aroma of damp needles drying in the sun fills the forest with anticipation. But the sun loses ground, the great clouds billow, and a fresh snow drives all apparent signs of spring down again beyond the ponderosas and incense cedars.

Not all gains are thus lost, however. In the stream channel the water runs a little deeper. Along its banks the alders are pushing forth their tassels, and within the willow buds tiny cells are dividing. The days are slightly longer than they were a week before, and life's inner substance is impatient.

Warm days persist, clouds and snow flurries diminish; sporadically but perceptibly, the

snowpack recedes. Drifts shrink back from the sun and find a last refuge in the denser groves of firs.

The forest comes alive with the sound of water. Faint gurglings develop beneath the snow where meltwaters drain into a common channel. Unseen but audible, the little trickles gather, pushing and thawing downslope, carving tunnels through the pack until they burst forth at the edge into the sunlight.

I explored a number of these snow caves one spring morning in a forest clearing beside the creek. The first dip beneath the pack was the hardest part of the journey, for though my hands and feet were already wet my belly was not, and the ice water draining from the tunnel was startlingly cold. I was soon enough numb all over and free to slither like a giant salamander through the burrows of spring thaw.

Inside, the brilliant glare of sun and snow was transformed. I had entered an altogether different world, secret realm of the buried meadow, hidden source of the river. Beneath me, flattened and spent, were last year's grasses and soggy sedge blades. Somewhere underneath, the seeds and living roots were preparing their sprouts. A thin trickle of water flowed around me, released at last from the ice chains of winter.

I rolled over on my back and studied the snowpack above me. The walls and ceiling were irregular and rippled. Through the filter of ice the sunlight shone in shades of blue and turquoise, as though some mysterious, heatless phosphorescence had been kindled. Strange, concentric lines were drawn around concavities in the ceiling like onion rings or contour lines of a topographic map. They were growth rings of the snowpack, a record of every storm

*Opening the stores is the first task of spring.*

and freeze throughout the winter, written for no one to see but the dormant meadow in its tomb, just another story that water tells in its immense and endless cycle.

I crawled ten feet deeper into the pack, until the pale blue light dimmed and the tunnel divided, preventing my passage. There, half embedded in the cave wall, I found a fir sapling. I had reached the edge of the forest.

I backed out and emerged into blinding, warm sunlight, rather unsure where I had been. Was it simply an odd spelunker's dream? Had I found the source of the river? Or had I visited the Emerald City? After exploring several more snow tunnels, I finally concluded that the Wizard of Oz was really water itself, which builds many incredible things in the course of a season. But for all the splendor of blue ice walls, the water still tasted like mountain water, cold and sweet. I took a long drink, thawed myself a while on a sunlit rock, then followed the meltwater downstream.

Ahead in the distance the forest resounded. The main stream course lay around a rocky bend, and I quickened my pace. Shortly I was standing beside a raging cataract; the roar was incessant, deafening, enveloping. Great bursts of spray sprang up against the granite, and the mountains fairly trembled.

The firs stood back and away from the water, but the alders and willows braved the torrent, for they belong to the stream and must take what it offers. The alders gripped the granite firmly, defying the flood, resisting the grinding, tearing forces which raged around their roots. High above the stream their twigs were leafing in the sun, drawing water from the noisy flow for use in the silent chemistry of photosynthesis.

The willows, however, would have to wait for their chance at spring. Growing low on the stream banks, they were nearly buried in the scouring flood, whipped and battered, still naked, their tender leaves still encased in protective bud scales.

I marveled at their durability and their strength, and even at their patience, if plants can be said to possess such an attribute. As I watched them being flailed relentlessly, I puzzled over the thought that perhaps no benefit in nature, not even a chance to live beside a mountain stream, is gained without sacrifice.

I swung by a root to a narrow ledge and inched my way beneath an arch of spray. The stream was the whole world, crashing wildly about me, pounding down the canyon at the insistence of gravity. This was the great release, the surge of energy which all living things anticipate in the spring. It was frantic, untamed, enough to cause heart pound, blood rush, and a shiver even in the forest.

The stream was in full splendor, emerging from snowdrifts and icy ponds, with a zillion sources in the forest and beyond timberline, in the heavy clouds of winter and the sea from which they came—the ocean reservoir that supplies and receives. I could feel in the coursing of my blood that this was the cycle flowing, slow in winter, fast in the spring, water on the move, a journey with no beginning and no end. It was a cycle of millennia, a year, or a moment, the cycle of glaciers, a stream, or blood flow in a gnat. This was the water of life.

I stayed with the stream all afternoon, receiving its spray, drinking its water, exploring the bouldered banks and twisted roots which held the mad flow in.

The stream entered my system like a transfusion. I had been insulated most of the winter,

*Water on the move —a journey with no beginning and no end.*

The melting of the snowpack is
a great release, a surge of energy
which all living things anticipate
in the spring. The stream becomes
frantic, untamed, enough to cause
heart pound, blood rush, and
a shiver even in the forest.

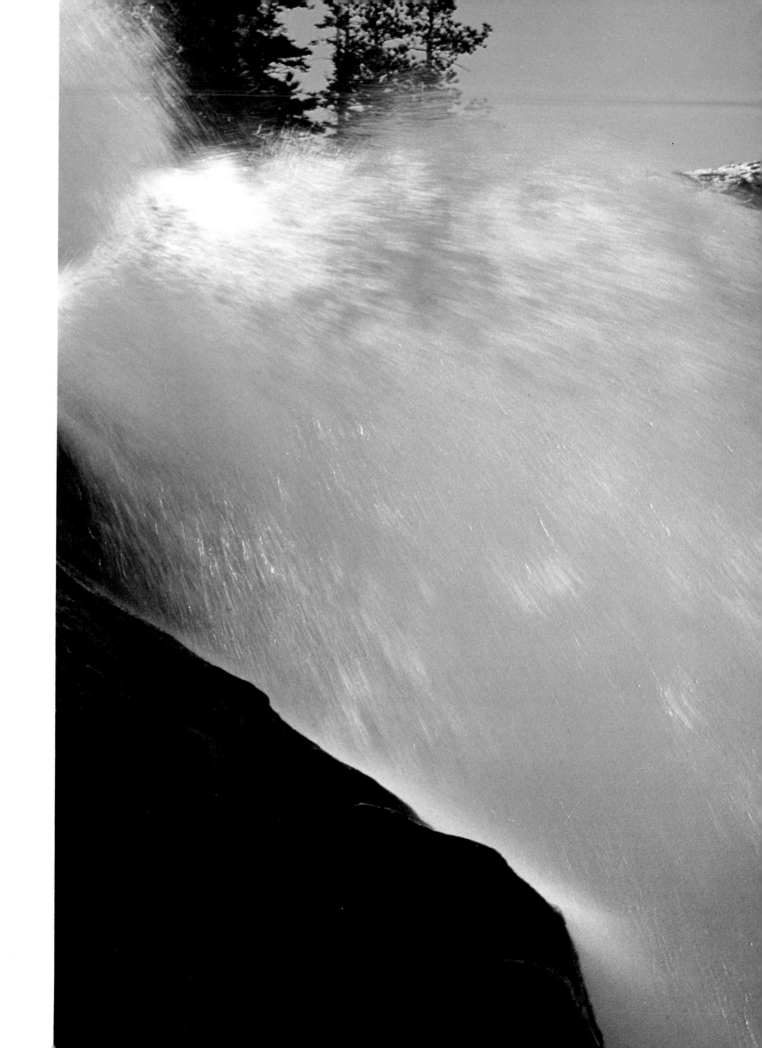

waking up in a warm house, moving about in the womb-like envelopes of civilization, living the easy life we have learned to expect of our technology. The stream was like opening a window in a room full of stale air—pure, alive with energy, and close to the source.

Even apart from our comfortable trappings, I think we tend to avoid confrontations with nature. We shun her wilder moments. A quiet meadow or a windless day at the beach are more to our liking than the meadow during a torrential rain or the coast when the storm surf is crashing. But underneath our hesitation lies the itch for excitement, a desire to share in something uncontrollable and infinitely more powerful than ourselves. This was what the stream offered, and by staying with it I encountered the brave pioneers.

They were growing in every little gully feeding the stream, pushing up through frigid currents, facing straight into the sun and spray. Far from shunning the rampant thaw, they were leaping right up through the midst of it, pioneering on the edge of spring.

They were the corn lily sprouts, infant hound's tongues, the shoots of sedges and grasses. They were the earth, the sun, the sky, and the snowbank transformed, fresh like the stream, participating, not avoiding, responding in order to survive.

Together with the alders and firs, they were holding back their share of the melting snow, siphoning off the precious fluid to fulfill the needs of their protoplasm. Embedded in the matrix of the soil, their roots would help to retain enough water to last them the summer and slowly feed the stream as well.

I have heard that wherever there is a stream in these mountains one is sure to find the water ouzel. I have never been disappointed, least of all that raging, thawing day of spring. Here and there I heard their joyous song, a melody perfectly fitted for a stream's accompaniment. These dusky dippers sing at their best when the streams are running full and nesting season is approaching.

For a long while I watched one feed, holding my breath and gripping the bank for fear the little bird would be swept away in the frothing current. But the apprehension was purely my own; after each dive for the juicy nymphs which thrive in these rapids, up he would pop, dry and safe, bobbing jubilantly. Here was a pioneer of another order.

Huge boulders were grinding slowly down the stream channel; gravel was in the making. The substance of the mountains themselves was on the move, and yet there was room enough in the scheme of things for a delicate little bird to dive for water nymphs, and time enough for a creature of the air to evolve this incredible ability.

*The stream is alive with energy and close to the source.*

*In every little gully feeding the stream, leaping right up through the midst of the rampant thaw, facing straight into the sun and spray, grow the brave pioneers of spring.*

74

*All things come to rest sooner or later. When the snowpack is gone
from the forest, the mountain stream runs quietly in its channel.*

*The water takes on a summer character, lazy and slow,*
*strung like wafting silk over little falls and cascades.*

*Here and there the stream rests in quiet mirror ponds.*

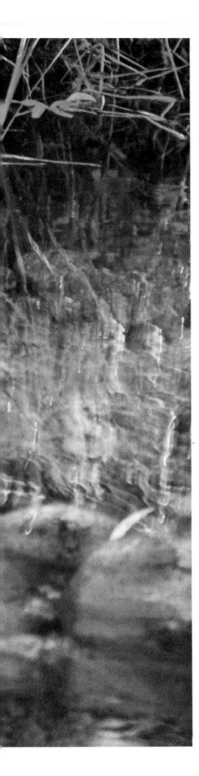

I suppose all things come to a rest sooner or later. Even streams run low on fuel, as stars and campfires do in their own time. When the snowpack is gone from the forest, the mountain stream runs quietly in its channel. Valleys and canyons no longer echo the roar of spring floods. Willows no longer bend beneath the surging torrent; they are finally allowed their leaves and flowers.

The stream takes on a summer character, lazy and slow, strung like wafting silk over little falls and cascades. It murmurs softly over slick granite and gurgles among boulders left behind by the spring rush of meltwater. Here and there the cold, pure water rests in quiet mirror ponds that reflect cliffs, trees, and clouds, or tumbles into aquamarine pools sparkling with silver bubbles rising.

Summer is a quiet time for the stream, yet it flows steadily on, fed by snowfields which persist in the shadows of peaks beyond timberline, by thunderstorms which crack and roll from the billowy cumulus, and by the slow seep of water held back in the soil for summer use.

If timberline is life reduced to the marrow, the stream is life's fluids coursing from the mountain skeleton, as our own blood is restored in the marrow of our bones. The stream is a great artery supplying the fir tree, the mistletoe which clusters in its crown, the birds which feast on the mistletoe berries, and the hawk which preys upon the birds. It supplies the deer browsing in the meadow, and the fly grubs which feed, after it dies, on the deer's carcass, and the many other creatures which in turn feed on flies.

Below the meadow it joins with the river and makes its final plunge toward the valley and the distant sea.

*Even streams run low on fuel.*

*Rich collections of lupines, larkspur, and tiger lilies
stand right up against the banks of the stream, conquering
the crystal water with their reflections. Damselflies and frogs
add color and chorus to the easy flow of summer.*

It is really only the water that moves on away from the mountains, what part of it manages to escape a multitude of thirsts along the journey. The stream itself stays where it is, etched into the mountain slope, altering its position no faster than the pace of geologic time will allow. For the plants and animals along its banks and beneath its surface, the stream is always there, dependable and essential.

Aside from the water ouzel, I know very few of the birds which frequent the stream, and there are many. I recognize the footprints of deer, bear, and fox, and I have been visited in camp some nights by coyotes on their way to the stream for a drink. What smaller mammals scurry among the willow clumps I can only guess about as yet. But the insects and plants I know as old friends, for entomology and botany have been hobbies of mine as far back as I can remember.

I know the big leaf maples, poplars, alders, and willows that arch over the water, casting the stream in eerie green dawn light even at midday, and the wild azaleas that fill the groves with fragrance when they bloom. My favorite mountain companions are found in little gardens, usually situated, it seems, in a spotlight of sunrays filtering through the tree branches. No two are ever alike, but they almost always display a rich collection of lupines, larkspur, and tiger lilies, standing right up against the banks of the stream, conquering the crystal water with their reflections, blooming lavishly beneath the rustle of aspens quaking.

Around the shady seeps which ooze all summer from the stream banks, ferns and horsetails spread their fronds, blue-green algae cluster, mosses and liverworts send up their spore cases, and an occasional mushroom or bracket fungus emerges from a damp limb. These are the water-loving primitives of the plant kingdom, tied by the needs of their reproductive cycle to the availability of free water.

In many such damp recesses I have found the tiny gametophytes of ferns, second half of their life cycle, the sort of minutia one wants to hunt for in an effort to appreciate the past. They are tiny green filmy things, a quarter of an inch or less across, and only a couple of cells thick. They are what spores become when they germinate on a moist bank, and they produce the sex cells which unite to form the embryos of new ferns. When water flows around them, even one drop of rain or dew, sperm cells are released from their under surface and swim until they find an egg cell, or perish in the process.

The journey may have been a thirty-second of an inch or a fraction more, but without free water the essential link would have been broken. Survival itself is contained in a single drop of water. Once fertilization takes place, the embryos enlarge, send their first frail fronds toward the sun, roots into the soil, and thus gain their independence. The gametophytes wither, their function fulfilled.

Once, when climates of the world were wetter and milder than they are now, ferns, horsetails, and clubmosses were the forests. Their tale is told in coal beds and fossil-bearing strata, but their evolution is illustrated no less clearly here beside the stream. Conifers and flowering plants have taken over the world. They have wrested dominion of forest and stream garden from the spore-bearers, reduced them to the status of dwarves, but on the shady bank the diminutive primitives persist. Here within the sweep of an eye all the phyla of the plant kingdom that have ever evolved are represented.

The insects, too, speak of the long road trav-

*For life along its banks, the stream is essential and dependable.*

eled from the ancient fern swamps. Among the uncountable billions of winged insects that lived and died during the past 250 million years, a meager collection has been preserved in the fossil record. The rest of their story appears in the structure and growth patterns of those groups which have survived the ages with little change.

The dragonflies that dart across pools hunting insects on the wing, stoneflies that scurry among willow thickets, and mayflies dancing in sunbeams over the water are old as flying insects go. To an entomologist they appear, in a sense, as modifications of the cockroach, the first animal that took to the air, that still retains the most primitive body plan of all winged insects. Like the cockroach, these ancient insects of the stream grow from nymphs, which look much like adults without wings.

Unlike cockroaches, however, their young live in water, strange crab-like creatures which cling to rocks in the rapids, or prowl along sandy bottoms, breathing with gills in the oxygen-rich mountain water. Some are predators, some scavengers, but all are among the preyed upon, for in the shadows hungry trout are lurking, and the water ouzel has young to feed.

In the stream shallows caddis fly larvae are crawling, dragging their protective dwellings with them. They are master carpenters and masons, constructing beautifully fitted houses from sticks or needles or particles of sand, selecting from stream-bottom debris only those building materials which suit the genetic blueprint of their species. They are newcomers in the stream of time. Unlike the nymphs of the dragonfly, these are larvae, worms we might call them if we saw such things in an apple. Adult caddis flies look much like moths, their closest relatives, and like a moth's caterpillar, their larvae must rest in a dormant stage in order to make the incredible transformation from worms to winged adults.

The bees and butterflies which visit flowers in streamside gardens, the yellow jackets which gnaw on old willow stems for paper-nest makings, the carpenter ants which tunnel unseen in a fallen log, and the mosquitos emerging from a stranded puddle are all modern insects. They are the conifers and flowers of the insect world. When a dragonfly devours a mosquito, somehow a great gap in time is bridged.

Aside from the hum of flying things and the occasional cricket song, the insect throngs are quiet. The frogs, however, are not; the chorus of their many voices often rivals the tumbling water music itself. John Muir found great comfort in their "cheery tronk and crink," and little wonder! One would have to look far for a more pleasant product of the stream.

Yellow maple leaves, just a few at first, record the sun's gradual shift to the south. Bears busily gather berries, roots, and grubs, their winter fat bulging. The pace of autumn quickens, the golden trees blaze. There's a nip in the air, and the first light snows have appeared at timberline. The stream runs more quietly than it has all summer.

Another season cycles past, but the stream flows on and on, through many seasons and many centuries, embraced by the meadow in its turn, and the sea and clouds in theirs, and man in his.

*The pace of autumn quickens; the golden trees blaze.*

*Another season cycles past, but the stream flows on and on, embraced by the meadow in its turn, the sea and clouds in theirs, and man in his.*

# IN THE MEADOW
## the seasons ebb and flow, while many smaller rhythms roll like waves through the grass

In the meadow, many things are always happening: seeds being shed, frost forming, snow falling, thawing, flooding; green plants making food, flowering; insects chewing, pollen-gathering, mating, laying eggs; birds nest-building, grub-hunting, rearing their young; ponds filling, trees encroaching. It's a landscape on the move, diverse, busy, and full of surprises.

The processes at work in the meadow are the same as they are everywhere there is life, but they somehow seem more compressed, gathered into a single fold. The meadow, for me, is a symbol of all relationships in nature, the story of ecology in a richly bound edition.

Come out on a spring morning, set aside the concerns of the city. Put your ear to the melting snow. Listen to the water trickle, feel the lift of the breeze, watch the clouds gather. Imagine a thousand seeds, a thousand separate organisms beneath your body, awakening to a new season.

Lie flat beneath the summer sun, your face in the grass, and watch a dozen visitors come to a single flower. Then count the flowers. Come when the aspens are turning, when the grass is rust-red at sunset and blue with frost at dawn.

For once let the meadow be the center of your world. It does something for your body and your spirit; you will not leave the same as you were when you arrived.

You will see things dying and being born, feeding and being fed upon, producing and consuming. You will catch a glimpse of nature's superb economy. You may never again be satisfied with bad air and fouled water, too much garbage and too many people, if you find in the meadow the meaning of balance. At the very least you will know that you are not alone in your striving after the needs of life, for beneath your body as you lie in the meadow are those thousand seeds also working to stay alive.

*A meadow is the story of ecology in a richly bound edition.*

*When grasses turn brown and the seeds are cast, the meadow lies still and quiet, waiting for winter.*

Frost is the fringe of winter, a borderline creation that forms on leaf margins at the edge of dawn. Someone must watch it building, perhaps the wandering coyote or the red fox hunting berries where the forest gives way to the meadow. But for day creatures like ourselves, the frost is simply there, a product of some night magic we understand only as the coming of the cold.

Frost is a special seasonal bonus for those who rise with the dawn. I remember it from childhood as a thick white stubble, a hoary night beard grown upon the bridge planks, good for an exhilarating running slide, or for scraping up into "flatlanders' snowballs," as we used to call them. In my neighborhood it was the only substitute we had for snow.

Over the years I have developed a deeper appreciation for frost; I would rather watch the sun erase it than plow it up with my shoes. Perhaps the fascination comes from the fabulous diversity of form and design, or from the vague understanding that frost, like snowflakes, reflects the unseen molecular structure of water. Each kind of leaf gathers frost differently, according to its shape or the arrangement of its surface hairs. Old seed stalks and spider webs add their touch of variety. Particular conditions of moisture and temperature may alter the scene completely, creating a thin white mantle one night and a monstrous growth of superfrost the next, covering even the leaves of tall trees.

A touch of magic may lie also in the ephemeral nature of frost. That such incredible structures can be engineered in the course of a night and torn down again each morning may seem at once admirable and wasteful to us, for man has a sense of history and tends to cherish his monuments. Water, however, which has a history infinitely older and more amazing than our own, is unmindful of these matters.

In the mountain meadow, water is never wasted. When frost melts, its entire substance is soon enough used somewhere else. What water escapes the grass-roots grasp of the meadow nourishes an earthworm, provides a beetle with a morning drink, or joins the clouds.

Some of it may soon fall again with the first snow. For many weeks of autumn the frost gives warning. Willows respond with a golden blush, seeds strengthen their protective coats, roots and rodents gird themselves for an underground hibernation. In the foothills, grass seeds wait for the first rain. Timberline lakes are laced with ice. Tropical forests near the equator are enjoying their customary afternoon cloudburst, while in temperate latitudes of the Southern Hemisphere the first spring wildflowers are blooming. The sun and the water give their signals in their own time. Here in the mountain meadow the time has come for the first snow, as it has every autumn since the retreat of the

*Frost is the fringe of winter,*
*a borderline creation that forms*
*on leaf margins at the edge of dawn.*
*It is the product of some night magic*
*which day creatures understand only*
*as the coming of the cold.*

*In the mountain meadow, water is never wasted.*

*How do spiders view frost
on their webs? As so much flotsam
cluttering the lines? Or are they too numb
from the morning cold to notice?*

last glaciers allowed summer again upon the slope of the range.

Snow piles up in deep drifts upon the meadow, as it does beneath towering firs in the surrounding forest. It builds layer upon layer, storm upon storm, melting and evaporating during warm days, compacting and refreezing when the nights and days are cold. Thirty to sixty feet of snow may fall during the course of the winter; of that amount about half persists through the winter to feed the mountain slope in spring and summer.

The earth slowly swings around the sun into another year. The balance between fire and ice teeters once again toward thaw, as it does at timberline each spring, or among frost crystals each morning, or even among glaciers in time.

As water flows from the snowpack, the heartbeat of life quickens. Even before the first bare patch of meadow appears, sedge shoots are pushing through the soggy mat of last year's leaves. As though everything alive were tired of the long winter, sprouts nudge impatiently at the snow, perforate the drift margins, and chase the receding pack across the meadow to the shady edges of the forest.

Without trees to intercept the warm sunrays, meadow snow melts quickly, running in sheets over young things growing, gathering in tributaries which feed the swelling stream. In flat stretches of the meadow, the stream spills its banks and adds its share to the melt marshes. Yet the plants push on, reaching for air, rising toward the sun, leafing, soaking up the water while the reservoir is full.

Finally the great rush of snowmelt subsides; the meadow drains, torrents shrink to rivulets, and the stream rests easy in its channel. Across the meadow lies a serene sea of green, rippling in the mountain breeze.

The time is approaching for the culmination of all this lush production, the zenith of life's striving after sun and water and nutrients from the soil. The reason for life, if there is one, must lie in the realm of self-perpetuation. That which lives only for the moment and not for the future has no future. In due course all organisms must create more of their own kind if they are to survive. The sun is high, summer has come, and flowers appear upon the meadow.

They come slowly, each species according to its own schedule. Even while the snow is still melting, tiny violets are blooming and shooting stars send up their pink, pointed darts. Their work is finished early, their seeds set and shed; but other flowers replace them, building color upon color until the meadow becomes a spectral display that rivals the rainbow.

When the meadow is in full flower, one can more easily appreciate the incredible diversity of living things in this single small place between the forest walls: corn lilies and cow parsnips, lupines, paint brush, blue-eyed grass, and several kinds of daisies; small blue gentians and diminutive sedges growing among the grass, and the grasses themselves blowing in the wind.

I have crawled through the meadow on all fours, as a photographer would with a camera, as a scientist would looking for an answer or a poet looking for an inspiration, as anyone must who strives to understand the workings of life. I have seen plant species by the dozens, and dozens more kinds of insects visiting them. I

*As water flows from the snowpack, the heartbeat of life quickens.*

have seen spiders, birds, and deer, the burrows of rodents and footprints in the mud of bears, coyotes, foxes, and raccoons. In the soil live a multitude of tiny spiders, mites, and insects, and a large parcel of bacteria, fungi, and protozoans which I know only from those who have studied such matters.

How many species are there in a mountain meadow? I don't know. And how many individual lives? I don't know that either; I have always been too bewildered by the immensity of it to make an estimate, though I'm sure others have done so. What I do know, however, is that I am one and they are many, many beyond counting, perhaps, if we include even the bacteria. I also know that I, one man, given the tools of my race, could destroy them all.

Meadows are good for many uses. They make fine pastures, good sites for highways, hotels, subdivisions, or parking lots. As a man in a strategic position, I could order any one of these uses into being. As a consumer, I could patronize the services offered by the results: a fine steak, a place to drive, to stay for the night or spend the summer, a space to park.

In either event, what would be destroyed? This we must know, for in every paved-over, road-graded, subdivided meadow, in everything we build and everything we consume, lies the stamp of our collective attitude toward the land and the life upon it. In the way we shape that attitude lies our future.

The meadow, even at a casual glance, is a complex community; one could spend a lifetime delving into its secrets and still not know them all. If we just look closely in a few corners, however, we can begin to understand what the meadow signifies, how it works, and what pattern it weaves in the web of life.

Flowers make a good beginning, simply because they are everywhere in the meadow, spring, summer, and fall, and they catch our eye first. What do flowers have to offer besides a splash of color and cause for a deep breath?

Flowers are part of the earth. They drink of its water and nutrients, they grow from it and return to it when they die. For the insects which sip their nectar, collect their pollen, or chew their leaves, for the bacteria and fungi which feed upon their remains, they are survival itself.

Like everything else which has evolved, flowers have a history, and in this case it is a history of change which profoundly altered the surface of the earth.

Back along the stream, growing secretively on a moist bank, we saw thin green gametophytes, the inconspicuous sexual generation of ferns. They were dependent upon the moisture they found there, for their motile sperm must swim through a film of water in order to fertilize the egg cells and thus produce new ferns.

The first spore-bearing plants were algae and fungi, and they appeared on earth perhaps two billion years ago. All the plants which followed for a billion eight-hundred million years were dependent upon free water for reproduction. Among them were the seaweeds, fungi, mosses, clubmosses, ferns, and fresh-water algae which still survive today, and many other groups of spore bearers which died out like old limbs shed from the tree of life.

Sometime during the Permian period, over

*The meadow,
even at a glance,
is a complex
community.*

The earth slowly swings around the sun
into another year. The balance between fire
and ice teeters once again toward thaw,
as it does among frost crystals each morning,
or even among glaciers in time. Meadow snow
melts quickly in the spring, running
in sheets over young things growing;
yet the plants push on, reaching for air,
rising toward the sun, leafing, soaking up
the water while the reservoir is full.

102

*The evolution of flowers profoundly altered the face of the earth.*

two-hundred million years ago, something dramatically new began to happen among the land plants. Spore-bearing leaves became more and more highly modified. In one of those great experiments which mark the most significant successes or failures of evolution, these leaves began holding the female spores instead of shedding them. Male spores were cast as pollen in great numbers and were carried by the wind so that some, by chance, would land among the female gametophytes growing almost as parasites upon the parent plant. There the pollen grains germinated, penetrating the female tissues and thus fertilizing the ovaries internally without need for free water.

After fertilization the male pollen plants died, but the female gametophytes continued to develop within protective integuments provided by the parent plant. The dependent gametophytes and the parent sporophytes were producing together the structures we now call seeds.

The conifers had been born, not all at once to be sure, for like all major changes in evolution, this one had been building by trial and error, step by step, for millions of years. Once independent of the need for free water in their reproduction, primitive conifers were able to survive where their ancestors could not. In addition, they had developed seeds, sturdy little packets containing embryos and ample stores of food to see them through the precarious times of sprouting and establishment.

It was lucky timing, for during the Permian great uplifts took place upon the continents. Mountains were built and climates became increasingly cool and arid. Swamp lands shrank and dried; the old swamp forests dwindled; across the new uplands conifers spread and

diversified. For nearly seventy-five million years they dominated the vegetation of the land.

During the reign of the conifers other important things were happening around the world. The Permian mountain ranges were eroding, the land was leveling off, and rain clouds were slipping through the barriers to water arid regions beyond. Reptiles were adapting to these changes; some groups, we know now, would become birds, some mammals, and others the reptilian giants of the next chapter in earth history.

The Jurassic period, age of dinosaurs and reptiles of the sea, extended for twenty-five million years. It was a quiet time. Vast lowlands stretched across the continental areas and climates were mild. The conifers still had the upper hand, but evolution was proceeding in certain quarters in a way which would have tremendous impact on the appearance of life to come.

The first true mammals and birds were developing, insects more like those of today were evolving, and the spore-bearing leaves of seed plants were changing even more than they already had in the strange cones of the ancient conifers. Somewhere among the trampings and chewings of ponderous reptiles over one hundred and fifty million years ago, certain leaves became petals, stamens, and pistils. The first flowers were born.

During the next seventy million years the earth was transformed. Great inland seas advanced and retreated, and once again mountain ranges were thrust skyward. Stimulated by changes in climate and topography, flowering plants adapted, invading every conceivable niche from marsh to desert to mountain top. Flowers were a new creation, bold and innovative; they inherited the earth.

Nothing happens alone in nature, for change begets change. No sooner were there flowers than there were insects to pollinate them and mammals and birds to feed upon their rich, nutritious seeds.

Before the evolution of flowers, the world had never seen a bee, a butterfly, or a hummingbird. Brilliant splashes of color and the sweet scent of nectar never existed in the meadows. Most of the conifers then, as now, were pollinated by the wind, and the wind is not partial to color or aroma.

Some of the flowering plants either stuck by the old system or returned to it, those with their tassels or flower stalks thrust into the wind. Among these are the grasses, the oaks and birches, alders and walnuts, and many others whose flowers are so inconspicuous we scarcely think of them as having flowers at all.

In order to insure fertilization, however, these plants must produce huge quantities of pollen. It is biologically a rather wasteful process; perhaps because of this, flowering plants have tended to develop specific relationships with certain animal pollinators, especially among the vast assemblage of insects which now inhabit the world.

Flowering plants have developed similar relationships for seed dispersal. They have evolved ingenious structures for traveling with nearly every agent of motion in nature—floats for riding with the stream or ocean current, wings and parachutes for drifting with the wind, hooks and spines for attaching to fur, sweet enticing fruits for inducing a journey within the gut of a wayward bird or mammal.

Just as the evolution of insects was revolutionized by the flowers, so was the development of birds and mammals. A new and highly concentrated source of energy was available in fruits and seeds, first from the conifers and then in increasing quantities from the flowering plants. There must be a very large number of animal species, including our own, whose existence is based on this rich source of food.

Mammals, birds, insects, and flowering plants, we can accurately say, evolved in intimate association. Together they developed one of the greatest systems of mutual benefit the continents have ever experienced. They have produced the world as we know it. Upon their mutual arrangements we as a species depend for survival.

All of this is contained in our mountain meadow. When you see a family of deer browsing, a bumble bee gathering pollen, or a flock of finches feeding on thistle seeds, you know the history is there, millions upon millions of years of it. And the story of water is there, too, the water that piled up against the mountains of the past, that coursed through the veins of every living thing which helped to write those incredible chapters of evolution, the water that fed the embryonic fires in billions of seeds which made the whole thing possible.

The story is told by fossils stored in dark museum cabinets, by books stacked upon dusty library shelves, but it is told infinitely better by the pulsing, teeming life of the meadow. Here the living roots of history are contained in a single flower. How, then, except by the utmost necessity, could we conspire to destroy it?

*Nothing happens alone in nature, for change begets change.*

105

When the meadow is in full flower,
one can more easily appreciate
the incredible diversity of living
things in this single small place
between the forest walls.

The beauty of history is that events which happened in the past still find expression in the present. No matter how lost they may seem in the mainstream, they are here now, every last particle of history, like single molecules of water rushing with the multitude downstream, each lending its weight to the nature and direction of the present.

Human history works this way as well as any other segment of the earth's past. Events which happen at this moment, patterns of culture which exist today, the things we do, the way we act—none of these aspects of man's past stands alone. They all have antecedents in history, though the connections with the past and the many pathways traveled through years and centuries may now seem circuitous and vague.

History also has a future, for time is a continuous phenomenon as far as we can see it stretching away in either direction. We predict the future endlessly. Perhaps the fascination we find in doing so comes from knowing that things may fall together in any one of an infinite number of ways, and from realizing that chance plays an important part in this process.

But we know also from studying the past that, in spite of the apparent randomness of nature, events occur and directions flow in strict accordance with universal principles. There are physical laws, and biological laws derived from them, which have extended through at least as much of time as our limited vision can accommodate. In learning what events have taken place in the past and how they may have brought the world forward toward its present form, perhaps man finds his only opportunity to understand with some perspective the principles which govern the universe.

*One blade of grass may contain all the earth's history.*

The evolution of life on our planet is one continuous historical sequence, a collection of events beyond counting stacked one upon another and all blended in one vast, flowing network. No flower in the meadow is simply a thing of the moment, for its particular floral plan, its color, its shape, the pattern of its growth, and the nature of every chemical which constitutes its substance, all have emerged from the meshwork of history.

The camouflaged crab spider that has captured its prey among the petals of a blossom, or the bee swift enough to escape the spider's grasp, or the tree that has set many seeds in a good year and none the next—each organism derives its successes and its failures from the past, from a great series of mutations and adaptations, a nearly endless parade of trials and errors, an assemblage of chance encounters the nature and number of which may forever remain beyond our knowledge.

In a single blade of grass a third of the earth's history may be contained, and perhaps all of it if we could only follow the story far enough back in time. Grass is worth considering, for it holds in its green blades a part of the reason why we and the rest of life have become what we are.

The mountain meadow is mostly made of grass, million upon million plants of it. When we walk through the forest our eyes are often raised; our vision runs among the high boughs where the sun is held, while we, our earthbound bodies at least, rest in a pleasant patch of shade. But in the meadow there is no shade for creatures our size. We cross it, walk through the grass, over it almost, and during a hot day are just as glad to reach the cool forest on the far side.

It isn't that we don't like the sun or don't need a bit of it, for in fact we do. Our metabolism has its own special uses for a moderate amount of sunlight, and our spirit certainly feeds on its brightness and warmth. But the sun doesn't do for us what it does for the grass, because grasses are plants and we are animals. Between us lies the tremendous gap which divides the kingdoms of life.

There is something in the character of man which strives to bridge the chasms of nature. The same desire which urges the spanning of a river also drives man's curiosity about a plant's special use of sunlight. Even now scientists around the world are playing in test tubes with the magic stuff called chlorophyll. It is almost as though we are resentful that plants—the forest trees, the lowly weeds and grass—can do something that we cannot do.

Lacking the refined tools of the chemist or cellular biologist, I have pondered this incredible fact in my own way. The mountain meadow is as green a place as one could find on earth, green even as a tropical forest if you once get down inside of it. I stretched out one warm summer day among the leaves and flowers, my face to the sky, and tried to approach the world as a grass might.

All about me the grasses, brackens, and flowers were reaching for the sun, arching frond over frond, spreading leaf and blade toward the sky. Beneath me, an unknown number of roots and microscopic root hairs, many miles of them if one added them all together, were probing the soil, drawing water and nutrients into all those rising, branching pipes and vessels.

This teeming, thriving little forest, I found myself thinking, with its roots a few feet deep in the earth and its leafy canopy a few feet up in the air, was life's only tenuous claim to this patch of lifeless earth. Nearby, the tall fir trees reached a bit higher and deeper; a hawk flew from one tree to another across the meadow, and even higher a host of tiny insects were being swept along invisibly by the mountain updrafts.

Still, from a few thousand miles out in space, all the meadows and forests of the continent would appear as they really are, a thin, filmy blush of green on a little island of crusty stone. We have seen this now through the eyes and cameras of the astronauts. We are beyond denying the awesome truth, that the mighty firs which soar above us, the grasses which envelop us on a warm afternoon, and all the noble monuments of our own construction are products of a delicate, living membrane stretched precariously between the molten core of the earth and the icy void of space. Life is an experimental form of surface chemistry; it happens only where earth and water meet air and sunlight. It is a borderline creation, like the frost of dawn, and may last no longer than frost does, by space time.

Here in the meadow, the living film was only a few feet thick, and yet it contained every ingredient of the vital chemistry, the most essential of which mingled quietly in the green leaves that wafted over me in a little breeze.

I fancied that I had roots soaking up moisture from deep in the soil. I imagined that I could feel the water rising through a million veins, feeding the leaf cells where the green stuff, chlorophyll, is kept, that my skin responded, as the laboratories of photosynthesis must, to the penetration of sunrays.

*Man strives to bridge the chasms of nature.*

109

Grasses, brackens, and flowers reach for the sun,
arching frond over frond, spreading leaf and blade
toward the sky. Life is an experimental form
of surface chemistry; it happens only
where earth and water meet air and sunlight.

But it was only a fantasy. My experiment had failed, at least in part. I walked away from the meadow as only an animal can. I had no roots here, only a wet back from lying upon a boggy seep. There had been no green in my skin except by reflection, and my face tingled only from a mild case of sunburn. The green light which had enveloped me and soothed my spirit was nothing more than light the plants rejected, the wave lengths for which they had no use.

The process of living works constantly to consume, tear down, use up energy. The single source for this energy is the sun, and the only place where it can be fixed in a form available for life is the cell that contains chlorophyll.

The backbone of every organic molecule is composed of carbon and hydrogen atoms. All the carbon of which living things are constructed comes from carbon dioxide, and the hydrogen is taken from water. It is difficult to imagine, but it is true, that the mind which marvels at the green leaf, the very brain tissues which have unraveled the mysterious process of photosynthesis, themselves had their origin in the busy green places where these two lowly elements are united.

Within every photosynthetic cell there are numerous small structures called chloroplasts, and they in turn contain particles known as grana, tiny membrane sacs which bear the essential molecules of chlorophyll. When sunlight strikes chlorophyll, the red wave lengths are absorbed while green light is rejected. Chlorophyll molecules become energized and agitated. Through the excitement of their elec-

trons an important event occurs: water is split into its two components, hydrogen and oxygen. Six molecules of water thus divided combine with six molecules of carbon dioxide, and six molecules of oxygen are liberated as a byproduct. Out of this basic reaction emerges a single unit of sugar, the cornerstone from which all the elaborate structures and compounds of life are built.

It is a very ancient process that extends into the far, dim reaches of time. As a child I used to stare, as I still do, into the grimy mud of stagnant pools, wondering what minuscule creatures stirred there. Many times I saw dark green patches of scum on the bottom, spreading over the mud in thin sheets. I have learned since that these murky splotches were aggregations of blue-green algae similar to those which have been found as fossils estimated to be two billion years old. These single-celled algae may have been the first organisms capable of photosynthesis, and the process has extended across the millennia to the present day with only minor refinements.

It was a far different world then. The atmosphere contained no oxygen, there were no animals, and plant life had not yet exceeded the form of a single cell.

But in those cells a strange chemistry was evolving, a kind of sun-driven chemistry that would produce free oxygen for the first time on earth. Bacteria had lived before without needing molecular oxygen; their respiration was based upon other pathways of tearing down the sun-built compounds. But as photosynthesis became more highly refined, respiration, that essential process of living shared by every organism of all time, became what it most commonly is in the world today—the breaking down of high-energy sugars in the presence of oxygen and the consumption of their energy. Sugar and oxygen, the products of photosynthesis, were recombined, carbon dioxide was released, and water, that incredible compound which makes life possible, was pieced back together again. The cycle was thus completed, and evolution assumed a new direction.

Plants began producing and liberating into the air more oxygen than they consumed. The sugars produced by photosynthesis were built into larger sugars and were garnished with nutrients from the land and nitrogen fixed from the air by special bacteria. Enzymes and starches were made, and a diverse host of additional organic compounds. New kinds of tissues were constructed which served new functions, and by them plants inherited the world.

This excessive plant production and the oxygen thus produced gradually gave rise to a great division of labor in the world of life. New organisms arose in the mainstream of evolution, organisms which gave up the chemistry of production and lived only by consuming what the plants created. From this ancient lineage has come the nectar-sipping bee and the spider that snares it, the bird that feeds on the spider and the hawk that eats the bird.

All the great food webs of land and sea have arisen within this system—all the herbivores and the carnivores that feed on them, the secondary and tertiary carnivores that feed on these meat eaters in turn, the scavengers and the decomposers. These are the animals that keep the balance, returning all the plant substances, step by step, to the source—carbon dioxide to the air, nutrients to the soil or the sea—and returning also the water which keeps the whole system flowing.

The only thing they cannot replace is energy, for this they have consumed each step along the way. So it is that a whole meadow may be needed to support enough insects and spiders to feed a large enough number of birds so that a single pair of hawks may provide for themselves and their young. This is the pyramid of numbers, a scale of diminishing energy. When they die, plants and hawks alike, and the decomposers are finished with the remains, only the nutrients, and gases, and the water from which they were built, are left. All that precious energy from the sun is gone, used up by the consumers, and must be replaced again by producers with the magic green stuff in their cells.

From this ancient animal lineage also has come man, and we are, so far, no different from the rest. We have grown rich on the plant foods of leaf, root, and seed, or animal foods derived from them. All the great productions of civilizations both past and present stand as monuments not so much in honor of man as in honor of countless precious kernels of grain.

"The human brain," Loren Eiseley has written, "so frail, so perishable, so full of inexhaustible dreams and hungers, burns by the power of the leaf."

*Photosynthesis extends into the far, dim reaches of time.*

*Within the cells of the tiniest algae, behind the walls of the green leaf, everywhere that the unique compound chlorophyll occurs, the sun's power is held and transformed. Every living thing has been built from the products of this silent, unassuming industry.*

Our dreams are endless, and maybe also are the possibilities for their fulfillment. Yet only at the most recent edges of our experience have we tamed rivers, split the atom, and built solar batteries. The rest of our industry is based upon those ancient legacies of green plants, coal and oil. Millions of years ago organic compounds produced ultimately by photosynthesis were locked up in the earth, and the oxygen produced at the same time was stored in the atmosphere. Now we are using up the stores. The wheels of our industry are greased with them; our homes are heated by them; we buy them in a thousand different products; we fuel our cars, our trains, our planes, and our rockets with them; we pave them over the land as roads and blend them as plastics. And as we burn them, we burn also the other half of this ancient inheritance, the oxygen reserves the plants produced in those distant times.

*Coal and oil are ancient legacies of green plants.*

As our industry grinds on and our minds play at the fringes of the impossible, we still eat what the plants produce and breathe the oxygen they give off as waste. Even our eyes feast on the soft green light the plants cannot use. For all its profound philosophy and awesome technology, the human brain, it is true, still burns by the power of the leaf.

The mind reels at the thought of leaves, millions of kinds which people the plains, forests, mountains, and deserts—broad kinds for catching the dim rays in forest shadows; narrow kinds, pinched and tough, waxy or hairy for resisting the parching heat and searing winds of the desert; round ones, slender ones; some immense, some tiny; some simple, some compound. There are even plants with no leaves at all, whose stems and branches are green instead.

Yet the same vital process goes on in them all. They must all spread their green cells toward the light and supply them with water drawn up through hundreds of vessels and veins from the soil. They must all provide pores and air spaces so that the essential gases can reach the cells and be given back again. An incredible diversity, leaves are, of variations upon a single theme, yet every one of them fulfills its function while meeting at the same time all the other demands the environment places upon it.

And beyond the leaf there are diatoms, single-celled algae, and giant seaweeds, all of which achieve the same end by more direct means, deriving the components of photosynthesis from the water itself without need for roots, vessels, and air spaces. There is undoubtedly more green surface area in the plankton and algae of the sea than there is on all the continents combined, and upon this vast wilderness of greenery we also depend in part for our food and oxygen.

Through all of these green things the water of life flows on and on, filling the tiny retorts so that the chemical reactions can occur, bringing nutrients to the leaves, splitting at the insistence of chlorophyll, providing the foundations for the molecules of all living tissues, carrying the sweet foods of photosynthesis through the veins of plants and animals alike, evaporating from pores to keep leaf and skin cool, transporting wastes, permeating cell walls, diffusing, dissolving, nourishing.

To add fifty pounds to its weight, an elm tree must use and give back to the air 1,700 gallons of water. An acre of corn will use 325,000 gallons of water in one hundred growing days. Two thousand pounds of the vital fluid are needed to produce and refine one pound of cane sugar, and five thousand pounds are used in the production of a single pound of wheat. How many pounds of plant material are consumed to produce a pound of meat, and how many pounds of meat have we each eaten in a year? If we would add these up, water, all too often taken for granted, would perhaps assume a higher place in our regard.

I thought about water, leaf, air, and sun as I walked away from the meadow. I walked through a green mountain world full of them, all four. Because of their special union, the caterpillar could make a living by the blade of grass, the bird by the seed, the squirrel by the pinenut, the deer by the tender shoot, the bee by the sugared blossom. Snails and slugs could rasp their way through life across the green leaf, bears and foxes could munch in season upon tasty berries, and scores of grass-roots scavengers could feast upon the dying stems and tangled fibers that were left behind.

I thought of the industrious pika of timberline cutting grasses and storing them for winter in piles beneath the talus. I remembered the alpine nut-gatherer caching his stores, and the pinenuts that germinated and grew through the centuries as a result of his foresight and imperfect memory. I thought also of the campfires I had built in a hundred protected alpine hollows and the warmth they offered on cold nights because a multitude of green needles had done their share of sun-gathering. I remembered that John Muir had written something about a campfire in the high country, and when I returned home I found the passage:

"The big resiny roots and knots of the dwarf pine could neither be beaten out nor blown away, and the flames, now rushing up in long lances, now flattened and twisted on the rocky ground, roared as if trying to tell the storm stories of the trees they belonged to, as the light given off was telling the story of the sunshine they had gathered in centuries of summers."

I remembered, too, crawling into an icy sleeping bag beneath the stars and feeling soon warm from the metabolic fires burning within my own body. Even this was the work of green leaves. My little meadow experiment at bridging the gap between kingdoms was not a total failure, because as I crossed again to the forest I grabbed a handful of wild onions and ate them. They were spicy and delicious. That night, when cool darkness crept over the mountain slope, I was warmed by the sun and the leaf.

Vision is not an automatic thing. We tend to see what we want to see. At no time was this more impressed upon me than one autumn a few years ago. I was driving through the country with a friend. It was a fine autumn; a gold glow was creeping out among the maple branches, the madronas were laden with scarlet berries, and occasional vines of wild grape blazed along stream courses.

We were quiet for a long while. Finally I asked, "Did you see the incredible crop of madrona berries? It'll be a feast year for the band-tailed pigeons!"

"No," he replied, "but there sure is a fascinating arrangement of transformers on these telephone poles."

I hadn't seen even the poles let alone the transformers. I was traveling with the trees, he with what man had made after the forester's harvest. We were on different trips entirely.

*Plants and animals live in balance as producers and consumers.*

Because of the special union of water,
chlorophyll, air, and sun, the caterpillar
makes a living by the blade of grass,
the bird by the seed, the deer
by the tender shoot. Snails and slugs
rasp their way through life
across the green leaf, and scores
of grass-roots scavengers feast upon
the tangled fibers that are left behind.

*Unexpected encounters may connect one more firmly with the meaning of life.*

We each have our own peculiar set of blinders which we wear to shut out the unpleasant or the unfamiliar. The commuter who drives the urban skyways without seeing the slums below him, the camper who lives in a trailer to avoid the spiders and the worms, the biochemist who has never seen the wild, living organism whose cells he studies in the laboratory—each sees what fits most comfortably into his frame of reference.

New worlds were never discovered, however, by staying at home. Wild, exciting adventures are available just outside our field of vision, if only we would explore beyond ourselves. Along the fringes of garden walls, beyond the edges of roads, beneath our feet lie unexpected encounters which may connect us more firmly with the meaning of life.

We are easy victims of the grandiose when it comes to the affairs both of nature and of men. We listen more readily to the proclamations of a high-level bureaucrat than we do to the quiet actions of someone doing one good deed. We see more easily a field of bright flowers than we do the happenings in a single blossom.

For all our oratory on the subject, we are probably farther from the meaning of life, on the whole, than children are. Some of this may be due to the simple matter of eye level. Young children are closer to the ground than adults are, they see more of the action, and, as a result, their eyes are often wide with wonder.

A large part of it, I think, comes with the fears which we learn and nurture as we grow older. A meadow, in becoming the known haunt of spider or snake, loses some of the appeal which it held for us as children. We stand to gain much from lying in the grass, from moving in close, from sharing a day with these animals so that we may understand that there is no cause to fear them. Only then can we appreciate, emotionally as well as intellectually, the vital role they play as predators in the web of life.

But it is best not to stay there too long lest we forget where we are in the meadow, and where the meadow is in the scheme of things. Standing back to gain perspective is something adults can perhaps do better than children. The person who sees with the widest vision is adult in his head, child in his heart, and lets neither gain for long the upper hand.

Once one has seen all that happens upon a single flower, a meadow never looks the same, nor does the forest once one understands the meaning of what goes on within a single leaf. The meadow could not exist without the flower, or the forest without the leaf. And the spider could not survive without the bee that it feeds upon, or the blossom that attracts the bee, or the meadow that produced the blossom. Nature is the sum of parts, and the parts cannot occur outside of the totality.

*Once one has seen all that happens upon a single flower, a meadow never looks the same. By moving in close, one discovers that nature is the sum of parts, and the parts cannot occur outside of the totality.*

Flowers are the crossroads of the meadow, busy hubs of activity where many paths meet. Based upon a few simple floral plans, flowers have developed every conceivable design for the single purpose of insuring their own perpetuation. They have struck upon a wide variety of advertising colors, and aromas both sweet and foul, to lure the insect pollinators, and many sorts of tasty nectars to offer these visitors as reward. All this splendid experimentation succeeded because the insects were evolving also, developing the special vision and the selective appetites which could respond to the varied flower signals.

It is a dazzling parade that travels the highroads and flyways of the floral world. Butterflies and moths probe the blossoms with their long nectar siphons. Wasps, flies, and beetles of many descriptions come also for a nourishing drink, carrying with them quite by accident a bit of pollen.

It is not by chance, however, that the bees gather pollen. Throughout their lives, as both larvae and adults, they are dependent upon the rich foods flowers provide, and stores must be assembled for the young. Solitary bees and bumblebees fumble among laden anthers collecting pollen on special leg or belly hairs which

On a warm summer day the flowers
blaze and the crossroads hum.
With much buzzing and flitting
the daily errands of survival
are accomplished and the floral
function is fulfilled.

*For all species,*
*timing*
*is critical.*

evolved especially for this function. And out of this wild apian evolution have come the honeybees, with their elaborate social arrangements, and honey itself, the stuff of flowers miraculously transformed for winter storage.

On a warm summer day the flowers blaze and the crossroads hum. With much buzzing and flitting the daily errands of survival are accomplished, the floral function fulfilled. And among the petals lie the predators, the flower-colored crab spiders and camouflaged ambush bugs which help to keep this essential system in balance.

The seasons ebb and flow in the meadow as the tides do in the sea, but within this larger cycle there are many smaller rhythms which roll like waves through the grass. All species come and go according to their own schedule. The whole meadow ripples with their variously timed appearance and subsidence. Each has its own season.

In the spring, shooting stars bloom while most other meadow plants are tending their first leaves. By the time they have gone to seed, the grasses are just shedding pollen into the summer wind. When the grasses have set their

*All species come and go*
*according to their own schedules.*
*The whole meadow ripples with their*
*variously timed appearance and subsidence.*
*Each has its own season.*

seeds and the bracken ferns have turned brown, the young grasshoppers, which have been chewing their way up from spring beginnings, finally shed their last nymphal skins and put on the wings of adulthood. As shorter days approach and the meadow seems on the brink of dormancy, the goldenrods burst into flower. The season slips away amid their brilliant spikes flickering like flames in the early autumn wind.

The waves overlap and pile up; their pulsing is the very heartbeat of the meadow. Timing is critical, for here, only less dramatically so than at timberline, nature employs its various economies. The flowers that bloom at dawn are visited by dawn-flying pollinators; those that open in the afternoon have their own special set of visitors. Flowers of the spring and of the fall are matched accordingly. Butterflies emerge and lay their eggs when their particular food plants are available, and their parasites emerge then, too. Wherever associations are drawn tightly, the waves of life coincide. And on either shore lie the snowdrifts of winter.

When the goldenrods fade the season runs to a close. The water from last spring's snow melt, which seeped all summer through the root mats of the meadow, has been spent, used in the chemistry of life and sent on its way. The stream meanders quietly, bordered by dry grass and old worm-ravaged leaves of corn lilies. All the pushing, striving, flowering production of summer is replaced by the ebb of dormancy. By the time the frost visits are regular, nothing green is left in the meadow; everything is cast in rich shades of brown, for these are the meadow's death colors.

Death is only a seasonal thing, however, the other arm of the balance, for the seeds have been cast. I have discovered this more than once in the autumn meadow; picking burs from socks and pant legs seems to be an inevitable operation in the fall. I pull them out and toss them back for a mouse to find or a spring sunbeam to sprout.

The old plant skeletons are beaten down with the first rain or snow. There on the ground they feed the tiny soil organisms and the bacteria and fungi which will finally return them to humus. Aside from the roots of perennials, only the seeds persist to carry on the species.

All the lavish growth of summer was aimed toward this single goal, the production of these dim sleepers, little flakes and discs and balls of dormancy, the nasty stickers in my socks. If you collected them from a few square feet, you could hold every species of plant in the meadow in the palm of your hand, and the weight of their importance would seem far heavier than the few ounces you were holding.

Their responsibility is awesome, but they are designed superbly for their task. I marvel at their tenacity, their stubborn refusal to submit to harsh times. Some seeds, especially those from the desert, may sleep for many decades and still not use up their small allotment of stored food, so slowly do their metabolic fires burn. They will germinate only when the right

*When the goldenrods fade,*
*the season runs to a close.*
*Aside from those roots which*
*live through the winter, only seeds*
*persist to carry on the species.*

*Seeds have*
*an awesome*
*responsibility,*
*but they are*
*superbly designed*
*for their task.*

All the pushing, striving, flowering growth of summer
was aimed toward a single goal, the production of seeds—
these dim sleepers, little flakes and discs
and balls of dormancy.

amount of rain has fallen in just the right sequence to insure their survival through the next round of flowering.

The food stored in seeds was produced by the agency of chlorophyll and sunlight from carbon dioxide and water. With the exception of what is linked by chemical bond in these carbohydrate foods, water is expelled from the seeds as they dry and shrink to their dormant condition. Only then are the process of respiration slowed and the food reserves conserved.

But when water returns through the seed coats and the temperature is right, the vital chemistry is kindled. Compounds long stored are mixed, chemical reactions long quiet begin anew, and the embryos swell against the walls which hold them in. In a drop of water, another season of growth is born.

Seeds carry with them the recombined genes of their parents, and possibly mutations which would make the species more or less able to survive. When the embryos sprout, they face the world with only what they have in their gene fabric. They are the pioneers of evolution. They hold the future of their race, unless we take it from them.

The meadow is part of a larger cycle, too, a rhythm beyond seasons. This broad grassy space between granite walls and tall firs was not always a meadow, nor will it forever remain so. Nothing in nature is entirely static, and certainly not the mountains themselves, though it may be comforting for us to know that they will appear tomorrow much as they did yesterday. Had we evolved with time-lapse vision, or a life span of epochs rather than years, we would of necessity be continuously on the move to give the shifting mountains

*The meadow is part of a larger cycle, a rhythm beyond seasons.*

and climates room for their wild pushing, buckling, and gouging.

"With our short memory," Loren Eiseley has said, "we accept the present climate as normal. It is as though a man with a huge volume of a thousand pages before him—in reality, the pages of earth time—should read the final sentence and pronounce it history."

On the one hand, it may be well that our vision, at least our daily view of things, is rather narrow, for we need some quiet bays for anchorage, some reliable hitching posts along our little journeys from birth to death. We must know that the sun will rise each morning, though we may understand that suns also are born and die in time. We must see that the mountains are there each year, with their windswept peaks, their towering forests and sunny meadows, even though the rocks may tell us of the mighty thrust of glaciers which only recently scraped them bare and smooth.

Yet on the other hand, we must know that these things do change, the mountains of today may be seas in another time, and seas, mountains; that the meadows we visit may be forests one day, and this even within the space of a few human lifetimes. We must also understand that nature's alterations occur slowly enough that at least most of the organisms imposed upon are able to change accordingly, or move on. Only by this knowledge may we temper our haste in changing the earth by means of our own industry.

Less than one hundred thousand years ago our mountain meadow was part of a granite pathway traveled, not by deer and dandelion seeds, but by a fierce river of ice. Off and on for a million years the glaciers had scooped and gouged, sheering peaks into domes and widening the valley. When the last glacier began to retreat twenty-five thousand years ago, the rubble of mountains lay crumbled and strewn along its former course. Some of this glacial debris was piled across the valley in moraines which held back the meltwater in frigid alpine ponds.

As the climate warmed, timberline crept slowly upslope; hardy pines braved the storms and challenged the barren granite. But they didn't linger long, for the climate to which they were adapted moved on toward the high peaks, and their offspring moved with it, seedling beyond seedling.

The pines left the pond shore a different place than it was when they arrived. The old twisted trees which stayed behind minding their roots gradually died and broke beneath the weight of winter snow. Storm-whitened logs littered the moraines and choked the pond. Wind and water heaped sand among them, and billions of needles and grass leaves and lupine stems, and seeds which made more of the same. By the slow process of erosion, growth, and decay, soil was built, and the pond grew shallow.

As timberline pines advanced upon the heels of the glaciers, hemlocks and lodgepole pines followed them, and in time they reached the pond. The place had been made ready for them; their seedlings took hold and they thrived. Their roots worked deeply among the glacial rubble, penetrating, dissolving, drawing up the deep-seated nutrients. Year after year for centuries they added cones and needles and limbs to the accumulating humus, and the soil deepened.

As the mantle of soil spread, the pond was filled inward from the shore, ringed as it was now by fallen trees and needle drifts. The hemlocks followed the front line of lodgepoles on up the slope and finally abandoned the pond entirely. The stream cut a new course nearby, and the pond was left alone among the trees.

A forest is a living, throbbing, building thing that works to heal the wounds of time. Streams are channels left open, old scars the forest allows to remain because it must. As long as streams flow, they have the upper hand; for though they may not win ground from a healthy tree, they can hold their own against a seedling, and they do. But ponds are retiring; what they cannot drown in their quiet soaking, ponds accept, and they die faster because of it.

Pond weeds advanced in the muddy shallows, their floating fronds growing and dying each year among old logs spraddled and strewn about the shore. Sedges, rushes, and grasses followed them in turn, colonizing as the soil built outward, sewing up the wound with their tenacious fibers and expert root stitchery.

Behind the bog grasses and sedges, following rotting logs to keep their roots from drowning, the first lodgepole pines made their way into the healing tissue of the marsh. Even while these adventuresome colonists were advancing upon the pond, new pioneers were arriving in the parent forest behind them. Fir seeds, blown up from their own forests below, were sprouting and taking hold.

In time, the old lodgepoles died and the firs replaced them. Only a ring of pines was left around what once was a pond and is now our meadow, the last scar tissue of the glacial incision. Slowly but surely, if climate permits, the lodgepoles will consume the meadow, and the firs will overtake the pines. If the climate warms still further, the story will be repeated among the higher mountain ponds, while the yellow pines and cedars will inherit the place where our meadow used to be. Should a cooler

*Ponds become meadows, and they in turn become forests.*

When the forest inherits the meadow,
or at least its former residence,
it creates by spreading shade and
falling needle a fresh new territory
for different forms of life.

climate prevail once again before the mountains are gone, down they all would come again, seeking their own place in the scheme of things.

The scene has always changed and always will, imperceptibly this way, seedling by seedling, needle by needle. Life, like every other facet of the natural order, is not satisfied with the status quo. Living things are constantly on the move, as the very atoms and parts of atoms are within them, restless and stirring.

The most interesting thing about this moving of life to and fro across the land is that each species inherits a formerly hostile environment, transforms it to a comfortable condition by the very process of living there, and finally, by the same process, changes the environment so completely that conditions are suitable more for another species than for its own kind. It is as though each kind of organism were fouling its own nest until it must move on, leaving the area ready for some other species which could otherwise not have survived there.

This is precisely the story contained in our mountain meadow. The timberline pioneers broke ground for the lodgepoles and hemlocks which followed them, while they in turn prepared the area for the firs. In the same manner, the pond became a meadow, one species succeeding another, each advancing on one side and retreating on the other, according to its own tolerances. The pond plants have moved on to other ponds by various means of dispersal, as the meadow species will before the forest closes in upon them.

Even now, when I return each year to the meadow, I can see the pines marching one by one into the grass, gobbling up the precious flowers with their shade. I know it is changing, and I know it must. What must not change, however, is that this place remain as wilderness, for only in wilderness can we see wild things

*On the forest floor, another form of succession takes place.*

living, like the pines, with their saplings in the meadow and their ancient monarchs fallen in a fir-forest grave. Only in wilderness can we come to an understanding of the time required to change the earth and yet maintain a condition of balance.

When the forest inherits the meadow, or at least the meadow's former residence, it creates by spreading shade and falling needle a fresh new territory for different forms of life. All the habitats are there for the plants and animals that evolved with the forest and whose existence is dependent upon it.

Ground herbs take their places among the needles; squirrels chew cones for fir seeds and pine nuts. Beneath the litter of cone scales they leave in their midden heaps, a new set of soil organisms sifts through the needle mat, continuing the essential process of building humus.

Brilliant tufts of yellow-green lichen appear on the fir branches, providing hiding places for forest insects and web attachments for the spiders which feed on them. The Steller's jay moves in with her mate and builds a nest in the boughs, while in old snags pairs of white-headed

*By the forest leaf that shades*
*and the root that penetrates,*
*the snowpack is delayed in its melting,*
*water is held back in the soil,*
*erosion is tempered in the foothills,*
*and in the valley far below*
*the farmer's crops are sustained.*

and pileated woodpeckers excavate their own versions of home.

On the forest floor another form of succession takes place in fallen trees and limbs, a microcosm of the same process by which the pond was slowly changed to forest. Soon after the green wood dies, the larvae of tiny bark beetles and much larger woodboring beetles begin their tunnel-chewing travels through the logs. They attract their own peculiar parasites, horntails and ichneumon wasps equipped with special drills for penetrating wood and depositing eggs upon their larval hosts. They attract also the bears, which tear open the logs with tooth and claw, and feed on the succulent grubs.

Carpenter ants excavate the fallen logs still further, and bracket fungi begin their work in the wood fibers. When the wood has been reduced beyond their preference, other sets of insects and different kinds of fungi and bacteria move in. Unlike the process which changed the pond to a meadow and then to a forest, always building and accumulating, the succession of organisms in a log lies on the other arm of the balance, the side of decay, working always to consume and tear down. But when these scavengers and decomposers are through, they have built one essential thing that only life can create: they have built soil.

The forest has its effects in other quarters, too. By breaking the wind and shading the ground, trees create a microclimate quite different from that found in a meadow or upon an open slope. By the leaf that shades and the root that penetrates, the snowpack is delayed in its melting, water is held back in the soil, and the drying winds of summer are broken in their thirsty forays along the mountain slope.

The stream is thus assured of an even, steady flow all summer; and because the stream ex-

*Every living thing borrows from the common source.*

tends far beyond the mountains, so does the influence of the forest. Erosion is tempered in the foothills, spring flooding and summer drought are reduced in the lowlands, the delicate balance of marsh and estuary is kept, and the farmer's crops are sustained.

These many things are contained in our meadow. The history of flowers is found here, the busy carrying of pollen, the setting of seeds, the snow and the leaf that provide, and the precise timing by which all systems function. The swish of grasses is heard here and the hum of insects busy on their daily routes. The meadow also holds a promise—the raucous rasp of jays, the booming of grouse, the hammering of woodpeckers, the chatter of squirrels, and the sigh of wind in the firs which one day will replace all that we now hear in the meadow.

All of them—the pressing shoots of spring, the deer that browses them, and the ticks that feed upon the deer; the beetle grubs in fallen logs, the wasps and bears that find them; the leaf that falls and the bacteria that decay it; the silt that settles in the distant valley and the farmer who tills it—every living thing borrows from the common source, the water of life that flows continuously in a beautifully balanced cycle of use and re-use.

One morning I sat in the damp grass, my back to the forest, and watched the coming of the sun. The meadow was silver with dew. From the tip of every grass blade hung an especially large drop of water, full and round. When I held my pocket hand lens toward them, I saw that each contained an image of the entire local world—the meadow, the forest, the sky, and the sun itself glinting through the trees.

The water seemed to be saying in these tiny

crystal balls that it is, in its own way, all-knowing, for at one time or another this same water has been involved in some part of every process that has occurred since the first great rains began falling and the earth was slowly cooled.

It has torn apart mountains and carried them, particle by particle, to the sea. It has dissolved minerals from the crust of the earth and made the seas salty. Sometimes with the help of the wind, water has fashioned all the sandstones, shales, cherts, and conglomerates the world has ever known.

It has experienced extreme pressures where the deepest rocks lie and severe cold among the highest clouds. It has been embedded in glaciers, exploded in volcanoes, and trapped for millions of years in the buckling strata of emerging mountains. It has gathered minerals in deep veins as ores and crystals, and has escaped in geysers or springs unchanged.

In the seas of long ago, one way or another by the special work of water, the first living molecules came into being. For two billion years water has remained responsible for the delicate chemistry of life.

Diatoms, uncountable billions of them, were fashioned with the help of water, their protoplasm nourished by it, the calcium of their shells drawn from it. In the water of the sea they were born, and there also they died, generation upon generation. Their shells were buried, compressed, altered, and uplifted again as limestone, only to be carved into caves of great beauty by the percolating, dissolving action of water.

Water did as much for the forests of ancient swamplands and the ponderous dinosaurs, nourishing them, bearing them steadily through life to a watery grave, helping the chemistry of every cell to store the energy which largely runs the industry of our own species today.

Water has coursed through the veins of millions of organisms we have never seen, not even in fossils. It has carried the sex cells of every plant and animal that has ever lived and within their protoplasm has made the union of chromosomes possible, for water is the river upon which evolution has charted its course.

It is the river of life with its source in the barren peaks and lifeless seas of the past, with its source again among the timberline crags of every mountain range that has risen since on the face of the earth. Water is the spring that nourishes the alpine garden, the stream that supplies forest and meadow, the river that feeds farm and city, and replenishes the sea.

It is the river that flows small through the walls of every cell, through the veins of leaf and limb, because the water hanging from the tips of every grass blade that morning in the meadow had come there just so. In the cool of the night, when transpiration was slowed and the air was moist, the roots continued drawing water into pipes and vessels which fed the leaves. More was taken up than the plants could use, and the excess escaped from special pores at the leaf tips.

But in those drops waiting momentarily for the sun, all of water's larger and smaller journeys were somehow contained, as the image of the meadow was also held for a brief instant in time. Water and life are two threads woven intrinsically together. They are the reason why I have written these words and you are reading them. They are responsible, in their peculiar relationship, for everything we are and all that we do, every one of us, including also the pine, the columbine, the chipmunk, and the bee.

I rose from my damp morning outpost in the meadow. The sun sparkled among billions of water drops, providing what seemed like an illustrated definition of infinity, but it was not

*Water and life are two threads woven intrinsically together.*

The water of life flows continuously in
a beautifully balanced cycle of use and re-use.

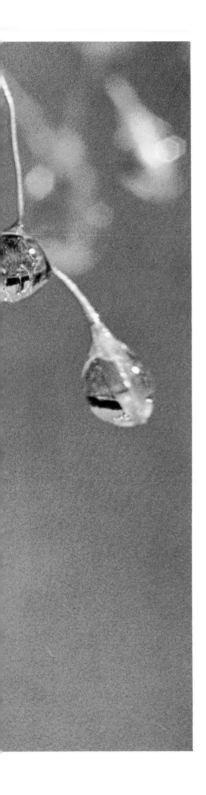

yet warm enough to dry the clothes I had soaked while crawling through the grass. If there was a time for the sun to accomplish the one task, I thought, there would be a time for the other and no need to worry over wet pants. The day promised to be warm, and besides, something more important was troubling me.

I walked to the center of the meadow where quiet water flowed between grassy banks. What would happen, I asked myself, if the stream that feeds us were polluted and spoiled, if the rain that supplies the river carried poisons from the wind, if the sea that receives the river were fouled beyond the tolerance of the life it contains? What would happen if the two threads, tightly linked these two billion years, came finally unwoven?

These events would have no effect on water, I realized, because water emerges from all its functions and burdens unchanged. It can carry poisons as easily as nutrients, garbage as easily as silt; and it will rise again as pure, clean water, just as I saw the mist rising from a field of dew that morning in the mountain meadow. For water, at least in this particular earthbound river, the end lies in the frigid palm of a dying sun perhaps billions of years from now, and in such a scheme the works of man mean very, very little.

But for life, what the water carries means survival itself. Water must bring to every cell only what those cells are able to handle, or the chemistry of life founders. The streams must run pure, the rain must fall clean.

Beyond the mountain, beyond the purifying, balanced influence of wilderness, the river enters the domain of man. It flows through the body of the technology we have created. When it emerges, it bears a new kind of chemistry with which life has had no previous experience. The poisons have begun to fall. There is no

*Life occurs in many forms within a single system.*

reason why they must, except that we allow it to happen.

When we return to the wilderness we cannot entirely divorce ourselves from our cultural trappings and the technology by which we created them. Even if we take our food from the land, we still wear cowhide boots and clothes made by machines; we still carry knapsack and bedding fabricated in some distant factory; we come by car from cities far away; and we light our campfire with matches.

We can no longer live as the Indians lived, totally in balance with the wilderness. We have lost the skills which the Indians had, though we could relearn them. Our expectations regarding time, food, and comfort have increased, though we could by choice reduce them. What is more important is that we are too many now, even as visitors, for the wilderness to support.

We cannot find our total sustenance in the mountains. What we can find, however, is our true source in the web of life.

We can see that life is a cycling phenomenon which occurs in many forms within a single system. Nothing stands alone—no individual, species, or community; no rain drop, snow crystal, cloud, or stream; no mountain and no sea—for in a cycle each thing in one way or another is connected with everything else.

The algae and moss, the shaded fern, the sprouting sedge and budding willow all draw upon the earth, the air, the water, and energy from the sun. In the green cell of leaf and creeper, a few simple ingredients from these four common sources are put together as the basic building blocks from which all life is constructed.

In the earth are found the various nutrients required for plant growth, the nitrogen from the air that was fixed in the soil by bacteria, and the water that brings these chemicals in solution to the leaf. This same water provides as well all the hydrogen atoms and some of the oxygen required for photosynthesis. From the air comes carbon dioxide, the source of more oxygen atoms for building carbohydrates, and the source also of all the carbon around which the complex organic molecules of life are built. From the sun comes the essential energy which drives this living chemistry.

The energy-rich productions of plants are tapped by the timberline nut-gatherer storing up for the winter, by the bird hunting seeds in the meadow, by the bee sipping nectar from flowers, by the larva eating old leaves in the stream, and the damselfly nymph that feeds on the larva, and the frog that eats the damselfly. In each instance the plant-built molecules are reworked to fit the animal's needs.

Finally, when living things die, the molecules are consumed again by scavengers and at last broken down entirely by the decomposers. With each use along the way, some of the energy stored from the sun is used up, until none is left. Only this energy must be replaced from outside, for everything else returns finally to the source—nutrients to the soil, carbon dioxide to the air, and water to both—at various times along the way.

We can't see these things happening directly, but when we see the green leaf growing, reaching for the sun, and dying, fallen and chewed upon the ground; when we smell the sweet scent of humus decaying in the forest; when we see one thing eating another and all things living together in balance—we know that they do happen, that they must.

If nothing more, we can learn from wilderness that this system is ancient and beautifully arranged. The multitudes of living things with which we share this planet have their own contract with the earth, and for this reason alone they must be allowed their chance to live. Their risks are great enough without our interfering.

But hopefully we can learn in addition that the leaf which feeds the worm has also produced its small share of the oxygen we breathe, that the woodpecker gathering bark beetles is protecting the trees from which we build our houses, that the stream with its source in the mountain snowpack runs through our faucets and waters our crops. We can learn from wilderness, by example, that the plants we grow for food and the pastures which feed our cattle need clean air and pure water just as wilderness plants do, and their soil also must be renewed.

We were born of the wilderness. Somewhere back among the glaciers of long ago we learned to tame fire and to make tools for hunting and for defense. Later we learned to grow crops, build villages, and domesticate animals. And then we invented the wheel and the forge. With each step in our cultural evolution, our numbers and our strength have grown. As our population has expanded, so have our needs, and the world has fallen before us.

This has been the pioneer condition of human civilization, spreading, consuming, burning brightly along its edges with the power of abundant resources. We have been dazzled by our dominion and blinded by frontiers stretching away to the horizon without apparent limit.

We have done all of these things in order to survive, but the tendencies we have thus developed were designed for lesser tools than those we now possess. We are able now to snip the strands of the web of life almost anywhere we choose, and we are doing so with increasing diligence.

*How long can man snip the strands of life's web and still survive?*

143

*We are voyagers in an old wagon embarked upon a new journey. We are like Stephen Vincent Benét's pioneers following the Western Star, saying: "We don't know where we're going, but we're on our way."*

# DOWN THE RIVER

*the water of life encounters an enigma—a species
that has, for the moment, forgotten the source*

*As the river leaves the mountains, it roars and tumbles
through steep-walled canyons toward the valley and the domain of man.*

Foothill canyons are the mountains' final hold upon the river. Gripped tightly by towering rock walls and steep, wooded slopes, the tributaries come together from many distant sources and join in a final, glorious plunge toward the floor of the valley.

Left behind are the clear, icy pools of timberline, the high snowfields, and shimmering reflections of the alpenglow. Gone are the giant firs, the green, flowery meadows tucked in their midst, and the rippling melody of water ouzels. In their place is the canyon, precipitous and immense. Through it flows the wild river, its author and its voice.

In the spring, when the snowpack melts and canyon days are warm, the river roars through the foothills, its rocky banks echoing and trembling with the voice of water. Trees of the higher stream hold firmly to the bank here also—the alders, willows, maples, and canyon oaks that grow at many elevations along the slope of the range, following always the river's course. They are joined as well by ash and cottonwood, trees of the hot valley and lower slopes that thrive with their leaves in blazing summer and their roots deep in the riverbed where winter snow water runs cold. Together, the trees resist the flying spray and grinding rush of boulders, but in spite of them the river cuts deeper into the mountains.

Here, too, along the narrow banks, are tiny canyon gardens, pinched and abbreviated, holding to their own cherished niches between the raging meltflow and dry, rocky slopes. They contain some of the rarest and most beautiful shrubs in the mountains—the spice bush, with its aromatic leaves and spidery, wine-red flowers; the incredible bladder-nut, densely hung with delicate, papery lantern pods; the snowdrop bush and mock orange, sweet-scented

*Along the stream's narrow banks grow tiny canyon gardens.*

and humming with insects.

Beyond the steep-walled canyons, the slope of the range is less severe; the hills stand back from the river and roll more gently. Yellow pines and Douglas-firs hug the cooler north slopes or drop away entirely, sure sign of hot summers. In their place grow hardy oaks and fields of grass, and on the rocky ridges elfin forests of chaparral stretch their thorny carpets.

These are the last foothills, rolling away toward the steaming valley in diminishing folds. Here summer rather than winter is the time of waiting. Only the oaks, the sparse, gray digger pines, and the woody shrubs of the chaparral stay green during the summer, their roots deep in the earth, their leaves tough and resinous and well adapted for conserving the precious water of life.

For almost everything else the season ends early. In the grasslands, spring begins with the first rain of autumn. Seeds sprout quickly and the new shoots toughen against the frost. When warm weather returns, the grasses bloom and set seed, poppies blaze on the slopes, and wild flowers of many descriptions put on their brief displays of color. Before the melting of the high snowfields has reached its peak, the grassland subsides into dormancy and waits there, scorched and golden, through the summer. Seeds are shed, insects go into summer hiding, soil creatures dig in deeply, and the buckeye trees, first out in the spring, already show signs of losing their leaves.

But along the river, spring is just getting under way. Cattails and sedges shoot up vigorously in the heat as the snow floods subside, and the delicate button-willow blooms from the boulder bed where only weeks before a raging torrent was churning.

Aquatic insects and frogs lay their eggs in

quiet pools, and at night animals come down from the parched hillsides for a much-needed drink. Deer browse along lush banks and raccoons prowl for crawfish or unwary frogs. The river canyon, this last foothill part of it, is an oasis in a summer desert.

"With rough passages here and there," John Muir wrote, these canyons "are flowery pathways to the snowy, icy fountains; mountain streams full of life and light . . . ." They are the arteries between snowpack and valley, lifeline of the foothills. For the creatures that come to them for food and drink, they are survival itself; for all those trees and shrubs, animals and flowers riveted by root and need to their cool, moist banks and clear, snow-born water, they are the only place called home.

Early one Saturday morning I packed some food in the car, and a sleeping bag, and struck off into the rising sun, bound for the mountains. I wanted a weekend away from the thick air and noisy traffic which had begun to wear on my nerves, and I thought just a couple of days browsing along a foothill river would restore my view of the world. I was sadly mistaken.

The sun was midway across the morning sky when I passed the first ripple in the land on the far side of the valley. From then on, the foothills rose gradually, fold upon fold, and the spreading blue oaks appeared more frequently. The trees were just leafing, the grass was still green, and the air was vibrant with the sounds and smells of spring.

I picked out the river on the horizon ahead, at least the green band of cottonwoods and valley oaks that mark its course. When I crossed the bridge, I glanced to the side and saw that the water was already high with runoff from melting snow above. I also saw that the water was muddy—more, I thought, than usual even for spring flood time.

The road left the river for a time and meandered on through the hills. When next it swung back, the river canyon had narrowed and the hills had steepened. My pulse quickened with a flood of memories of quiet river bends and intervening rapids, of giant cottonwoods and shaded gardens. I longed for a cool splash of water upon my face and the smell of spring things growing.

But when I reached my favorite place, I saw only ghosts of my old river friends, charred bones and open wounds. Memories would remain memories forever, never to be renewed, for between the canyon walls lay the foundations of a dam.

I left the car and entered the valley of death. High up the slope, above the future water line, a new road had been cut, and the scars were deep. From there to the edge of the river, and again on the other side, every living thing had been removed. The land was scraped clean; all the residents who had shared this peaceful place, the ancient trees, rare shrubs, every flower and blade of grass, were gone. Their woody bones lay smoldering in heaps, and the air was heavy with the smell of them dying. Near the river were the bulldozers, parked and resting.

Had those been people lying there burned and heaped, the perpetrators of this crime against nature would have been arrested and charged with murder. The whole world would still be trembling from news of the massacre. As it was—I read it later in the newspaper—when the dam was completed, all the officials from far and near were there to watch the last bucket of concrete being poured, and there was a great round of applause.

*The foothill river is an oasis in a summer desert.*

The last foothills roll away in diminishing folds.
Here summer rather than winter is the time of waiting.
Poppies blaze on the slopes, then join with the grasses
for a long, scorching sleep.

I walked on up the valley bottom where the cottonwoods used to be, following the muddy, gutted river. I could hear the grinding of rocks and gravel being rolled by the rapids, moving slowly out of the mountains at flood time as they have for thousands of years.

I found an old flood plain, churned up now where the tractors had been working, and I stooped to feel the rounded stones. There were granites here from the high slopes, some possibly from moraines left behind by the retreating glaciers; there were pieces of the ancient sediments and metamorphic rocks that were formed when the present range was still a thing of the distant future; there were smooth chunks of quartz, and I suppose, if I had looked long enough, I would have found a few flakes of gold.

These were the tumbled rocks of the river, the alluvium of centuries, born of the mountains and carried finally to the valley beyond as minerals and sand.

I thought of the Grand Canyon, the greatest river sculpture in the world. Seven hundred fifty cubic miles of rock have been removed by the Colorado in forming that one piece of splendid landscape. Dams, many of them, have been built on the Colorado; but in between, where the river is still wild, and along a thousand little tributaries, the ancient excavation continues. For the sake of expediency, we will have a little water for fields and cities; but in due course we will have only plains of mud and sand behind our dams. The river and geologic change are mightier engineers than those who have learned to pour concrete. They will win in time, even here in this small foothill canyon, but meanwhile the rocks will stay here where they are, and the silt that would have replenished the valley soil.

When this has become a lake, I thought, many people will come to fish and enjoy the scenery, and many more will gladly drink the mountain water that comes from their faucets, and wash their cars in it, and eat crops grown with it. They will know neither the lives it cost nor the uncertain future such luxurious tampering may bring.

"A living planet is a rare thing," wrote Kenneth Brower, "perhaps the rarest in the universe, and a very tenuous experiment at best. We need all the company we can get on our unlikely journey. One species' death diminishes us, for we are involved in life."

We need water, it is true, but we need as well the balanced river and all the forms of life whose existence is dependent upon that balance.

How many dams must we build to water more cities and nourish more crops in order to support greater numbers of people who will only demand additional supplies of water? How many wild canyons can we destroy before the larger balance slips from its fulcrum? This we must ask, because one canyon buried beneath a reservoir is more than one canyon destroyed. It is a delicately arranged piece of the larger whole, hitched to the mountains above, the valley below, and to the air and the rock of the earth.

*Near the river there were bulldozers, parked and resting.*

*The rock of centuries, born of the mountains, used to be carried to the valley beyond as minerals and sand. How many wild canyons can man destroy before the larger balance slips from its fulcrum?*

154

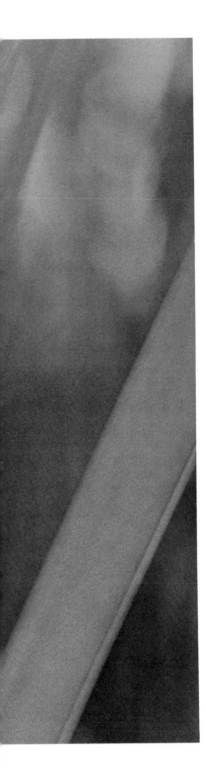

Beyond the last rippling foothills, the river enters
the broad valley on its final lap to the sea. When the Indians
had this land, the valley was an immense system of prairies
and marshes, teeming with game, visited each year by waterfowl
in numbers beyond our wildest dreams.

The air was clear, and the snow-capped range
stood out bold and beautiful against the eastern sky.
Through all this glorious country, the river ran
its jungled course . . .

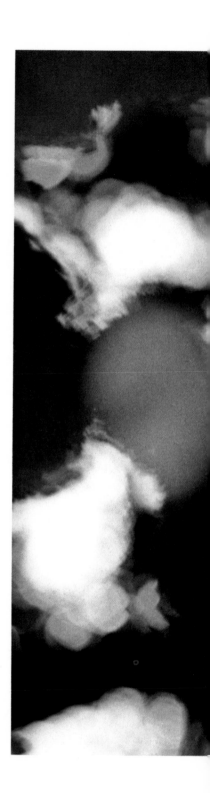

. . . *providing food for herons and egrets which nested here among the arching boughs, nourishing the wild grape which twined upward toward islands of sunlight among the treetops . . .*

*. . . bringing water to the plains and marshes, flooding them*
*with melted snow, replenishing them with silt and nutrients.*
*Now nearly all of this balanced life is gone*
*because you and I, and our parents and grandparents, said yes,*
*or said no and were not heard, or said nothing.*

When the Indians had this land, the valley was an immense system of prairies and marshes, teeming with game, visited each year by waterfowl in numbers beyond our wildest dreams. The air was clear, and the snow-capped range stood out bold and beautiful against the eastern sky. Through all this glorious country, the river ran its jungled course, bringing water to the plains and marshes, flooding them with melted snow, replenishing them each spring with silt and nutrients.

Now, nearly all of this balanced valley life is gone because you and I, and our parents and grandparents, said yes, or said no and were not heard, or said nothing.

We first sent the Indians away to reservations, what few of them survived our coming, and then we started on everything else that was, by our standards, wild and untamed. A few marshes were saved by hunting clubs, a few parks were established, and some tiny corners of wilderness have gone unnoticed. These widely scattered reservations are all that we have left, and even they are no longer completely wild. In the rich soil built by river, marsh, and prairie, we carved out some of the most productive farmland in the country, or in the world, for that matter.

We invaded, we conquered, we displaced, as the sedges did among the mountain ponds, and the pines and then the firs. Everyone judges that page of our history from his own vantage, and right and wrong are not easily defined. But we have done these things on a scale that no species of plant or animal, not even any previous race of man, has been able to do before. For this we must all answer, whether we are cottonwood, cattail, egret, or man.

Modern man is inexplicable, an enigma loose upon the face of the world. On the one hand, we have developed the powers of reason and objective evaluation to a level unknown among our ancestors. We have developed the process of scientific investigation, and from it we have gathered the greatest store of knowledge about ourselves and our world that man has ever known.

Yet by the same means we have developed a set of tools more powerful than our still limited wisdom can control. We are like children who have discovered rocks and windows at the same time, thrilled by the power and the crash. We are playing with matches, unmindful of the consequences. Who would have thought, just a hundred years ago, that we could split the atom, walk on the moon, or kill a lake the size of Erie?

We have cut the forests, drained the marshes, tamed the rivers, mined the hills, and farmed the valleys. We developed medicine, and by it we have prospered. Our numbers have grown by leaps and bounds, our cities are spreading, our highways and industries are on the move. Now we are re-invading our own farmlands, paving them over, building them under, gobbling up the soil of centuries, to accommodate our growing numbers.

Since the time we broke the first prairie with a plow, the spiraling imbalance has accelerated. When we replaced a hundred living species with a single crop, the insects worked away in the fields to restore the balance. We responded with chemicals and tipped the scale again in our favor. But insects breed rapidly, generation upon generation, and they soon developed strains resistent to our poisons. So we invented

*Man is thrilled by the power and the crash.*

161

The river once entered the salt marshes clean and rich,
blending fresh water with the tides, sustaining the
pickleweed and uncountable numbers of other living things
in the mud and shallows of the estuaries. Now the river bears
messages which the chemistry of life itself cannot read.

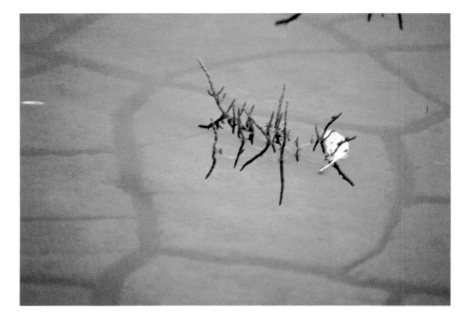

newer ones more toxic and longer lasting.

The poisons were blown with the dust into the air and began falling with the rain. They entered the river and were carried through marshes and estuaries to the sea. By the time the first birds died, the damage had already been done. Only then did we begin to realize that the insecticides we created were soluble in the fat of living cells, that they were taken up by plankton in the streams and estuaries, and concentrated along the food web as larger creatures ate smaller ones, until a fish-eating pelican had accumulated a concentration of poison many thousands of times greater than that in the water itself.

Now the pelicans, peregrine falcons, and possibly other carnivorous birds are unable to reproduce in many areas and may soon be gone. Fish as far away as Antarctica have gathered traces of insecticides in their bodies. People who work in the fields have become seriously ill, and some may have died, while most of us the world over have insecticides accumulating in our fatty tissues. Our solution to a single problem has worked against us rather than for us, and against the very substance of life itself.

We discovered coal and oil, a rich legacy of energy stored up from the sun by plants growing millions of years ago. We have made that energy work for us in thousands of different ways, and by it our might has grown. But in so doing we are poisoning the air we breathe and changing the delicate balance of gases in the atmosphere. When these energy reserves are gone, the quality of our environment will be diminished accordingly.

In another quarter, our playing with fire led to the splitting of the atom. Two bombs were required for us to see an inkling of the power we thus held at our fingertips, and yet the world contains enough peacetime and wartime nuclear devices, and enough stored radioactive wastes resulting from their manufacture, to kill most everything on this planet several times over. What small forms of life would resist the radiation, we do not know. We can be sure, however, that our species would not be among them.

"It is with the coming of man," Loren Eiseley has written, "that a vast hole seems to open in nature, a vast black whirlpool spinning faster and faster, consuming flesh, stones, soil, minerals, sucking down the lightning, wrenching power from the atom, until the ancient sounds of nature are drowned in the cacophony of something which is no longer natural, something instead which is loose and knocking at the world's heart, something demonic and no longer planned—escaped, it may be—spewed out of nature, contending in a final giant's game against its master."

All wild creatures on the earth live as part of a delicate balance. They take from the land, from the air, from the common pool of water, and from the plants upon which they ultimately depend for food. In the course of living and dying, they return to each all of what they have taken. Plants and animals have established, through the millennia, a fascinating partnership fed by the sun's energy and the richness of the earth itself.

Man was born a wild creature and has spent most of his years in keeping with the rhythms of nature. But we the people of our time are living in violation of the scheme upon which life itself depends. Since the development of

*As seen from space, our world is small and lonely.*

the earliest technology we have taken from the earth, in increasing amounts for increasing numbers of people, more than we have returned. We have poisoned the environment with substances to which living things are not adapted. Within a few short years, life on some corners of our planet will be largely untenable.

The quality of our air and water, our landscapes and our communities, the quality of life itself is being destroyed by people, you and me —by the cars we drive, the resources we use, and the wastes we leave behind. And what will replace us, as the forest replaced the meadow, if we create an environment unsuitable for our own kind?

In the normal course of events plants and animals move across the land, responding to changes in the environment and altering the environment still further by their own life processes. Over the ages, species come and go, only to be replaced by new kinds of organisms better adjusted to the conditions of the time.

But in the process of succession it is imperative that there are other places to colonize, and that in the areas left behind as species either die out or move on, conditions are suitable for the organisms which follow.

We have now seen the earth from space, and we know that our world is a small, lonely place drifting in a dark, frigid void. We are beginning to realize that when we have colonized the last corners of our planet, there will be no further place to go.

We are also beginning to understand that, unlike all other species this earth has ever known, man now has the ability to alter a place so drastically that when it is fouled beyond our own ability to live there, it is also spoiled for most other living things.

My father once said, and I have never forgotten it, that "man is interested in doing everything at once but unconcerned with doing a single thing with all his capabilities."

I feel now that the single thing man must do above all else is develop a balanced relationship with the earth, for this planet is our only home. Either we use it and cherish it with every capability, or life itself will lose its tenuous hold on this small part of the universe.

"For the fates of living things are bound together," Donald Culross Peattie wrote, "and a wise man can grow wiser, learning it. The perilous balance, the dangerous adventure, the thirst, the needs, the crashing end—they are impartially allotted to us all, tall man or taller tree. What we the living require is most of all each other."

Essentially, what we require is that when we look at a salt marsh we no longer say, "fill it, build on it, turn from it a profit," but say instead, "We need the air you replenish and the fish you spawn; we need the sound of birds calling upon your shore, and the expanse of your water to sooth our eyes and our spirits. Fellow creatures of the marsh, you are a part of us and we desire your company—you have a right to this place."

*Once we have colonized the last corners of earth, where will we go?*

*Here and there a few marshes exist undrained and unfilled. Let them remain so, for they are a part of the balance that man cannot afford to lose.*

The tides have begun to shift in the affairs of men. Seeds planted a long time ago, which have been struggling up through the shaded tangle, are finally leafing in the sun—just here and there, to be sure, but we must remember from history that all important ideas have a slow and often painful birth.

That man should live in balance with the earth is not a new idea. All the peoples we choose to call primitive have known this, and they have developed a myriad of built-in cultural curbs to restrain even what limited powers they have had which might have upset the balance. Their numbers were controlled; they did not go and come across the land too harshly; they learned to take, but also to give back. How else could Homo sapiens have occupied the continents for thousands upon thousands of years with only limited affect upon the earth?

It has only been during the last four thousand years of civilization, and especially during the last hundred years of the industrial revolution, that we have thought of ourselves as man apart and have behaved accordingly.

What we see happening now is a rebirth of an old idea, a finding again of something we almost lost. We can't go back exactly, for evolution flows the other way, even cultural evolution. We must move ahead, but only upon the ancient path.

The direction we have taken since the first great civilizations appeared on earth has been based largely upon expediency. The way that nature has followed—at least, we can be sure, since the beginning of life on this planet—this ancient way has been based firmly upon the principles of survival. These principles we also must follow, or we shall go down the short road to oblivion and take with us what other forms of life fall within our grasp.

We must first understand that we are not man apart. Like all other manifestations of life, we are made of earth, air, and water; we were built and are kept alive by the sun and the green leaf. We are part of the web of life and must respect the wisdom of its laws.

We can no longer afford to take from the earth more than we return in reusable form. We have mined vast quantities of metals, used them once or twice, and squandered them in city dumps or roadside ditches, at the bottom of the sea, or on the battlefields of numerous futile wars. We are still cutting forests faster than nature can regrow them or we can replant them. We are destroying precious soils, using them up, covering them over, a thousand times faster at least than nature can restore them. We dump and bury, or wash into the sea, our garbage and our wastes. We are creating materials that do not decay, that linger in the environment beyond the reach of life.

We must learn from the soil and the fallen leaf that the resources of our planet are finite, that they must be conserved and recycled. Only when we have modified our technology in accordance with this ancient principle will we once again reach equilibrium with our environment.

Nor can we afford to believe, as we have far too long, that a continuous rise in population brings prosperity to the human condition, that more babies mean good business, that there will be room enough for all and food enough to feed them. These notions are expedient myths, dangerous and devastating. The world is already overburdened, vast numbers of people are starving this very instant; this we could believe if we once refused to hide from their cries of anguish. The balance will be restored; it is only for us to decide how it shall happen. If we value human lives—as our religions, our laws, and our leaders constantly preach—then we must decide that the quality of life is the best way to judge the state of the nation.

We must learn what John Storer tells us: "The environment that supports life extends far beyond the vision or experience of the things that live there." We need to understand, now more than ever before, that one meadow altered is a million things affected far beyond the meadow itself, that a single change in a single natural system touches a thousand hidden corners of the world. We need to know more about our environment and about ourselves, so that we may more fully understand in advance the consequences of our actions. For only through knowledge do we see beyond the green leaf to the sun, through the shallow seas to the beginning of life.

We have just as much right to this planet as the pine or the chipmunk, the woodpecker or the whale—just as much but no more. We need, as they need, food and space and all the other resources required for a healthy life. We need some places for homes, some valleys for fields, and clean rivers to drink from. But we must take them only out of the utmost necessity for a limited number of people, because we need meadows also, as meadows, and forests as forests.

Until the coming of man, no wound was inflicted upon the earth that could not be healed by life in time. But we have learned from the earth's record that once a species vanishes, it is gone forever. New forms of life may cover the landslide or the slopes of a volcano, but those that are gone will not return.

With every species we exterminate, life itself is diminished. How many forms of life can we eliminate, how many poisons can we spread across the land, through the air and the sea, how many wounds can we inflict before life can no longer adjust and its very capacity to heal is thus destroyed? We must know these things, too, before we go too far.

Our aggressions have historically been aimed against our environment, toward some enemy we have seen in the glacier, the flood, or the neighboring tribe. But we are beginning to realize that in a society individuals must cooperate, and in the larger world community all of life must coexist in a state of balance. As we come closer to knowing how much we depend upon each other, upon the earth, and upon all the other species it supports, we shall find that our most important enemies are those which threaten our mutual relationships on this planet, and that those enemies lie within our inner being.

We shall find them and channel our aggressions inward; we shall thus conquer ourselves, each of us, inside where the marrow lies, instead of flexing our muscle against the world around us. When we have, we can look upon the sea and say in a steady, determined voice, "Life was born here. It has been a long road up from then until now. Here, life shall not die, at least not by the hand of man."

*We must learn to conquer ourselves, inside where the marrow lies.*

Life was born in the sea. It has been a long road up
from then until now. Here life shall not die,
at least not by the hand of man.

*In his total being—*
*in mind, body, and spirit, all three—*
*man shall find his final strength.*

All of these changes are starting to happen, because we are beginning to make them happen. We are picking up the tattered threads. We know far more about ourselves and our world than we did a hundred years ago, or even ten.

But knowledge is not enough. It is well that we have dying pelicans, stinging smog, and the memory of Hiroshima to remind us that it was through knowledge that we invented DDT, drilled for oil, and split the atom. Knowledge is a double-edged sword, and it is swung freely by the hand of man in either direction.

"The need is not really for more brains," Loren Eiseley implores; "the need is now for a gentler, a more tolerant people than those who won for us against the ice, the tiger and the bear."

The problem of man is unique, but so also are the abilities which we can bring forth toward its solution. These abilities lie both within and beyond the intellectual realm. They are to be found in mind, body, and spirit, all three. In this total being we shall find our final strength and a wisdom we have never known before.

Ever since we picked up the first stone and held it high against the world, we have been fascinated with the power of our minds and our bodies. With these we have learned to hold, not just a stone, but the very world in our hands.

But there is another part of being human, a part that man has strived to express since he first painted pictures of animals on the walls of ancient caves—beautiful, sensitive pictures that tell us more about ourselves than a thousand spaceships, dams, or factories will ever tell.

It is this part of us that loves the mountains and the sea; that listens for the cricket chirp, the quiet rustling of aspens, or the crash of the storm-surf; that marvels at the tiny egg of a hummingbird hatching or a thunderstorm being born. It is this part of us that flows with the river and the water of life, that tempers our extravagance and urges us to live by nature's carefully arranged economy.

*It is the child in us, the sense of
wonder, the compassion, that we are striving
for. This is the part of being human that
will guide us on our way and will insure,
this time, that we know where we are going.*

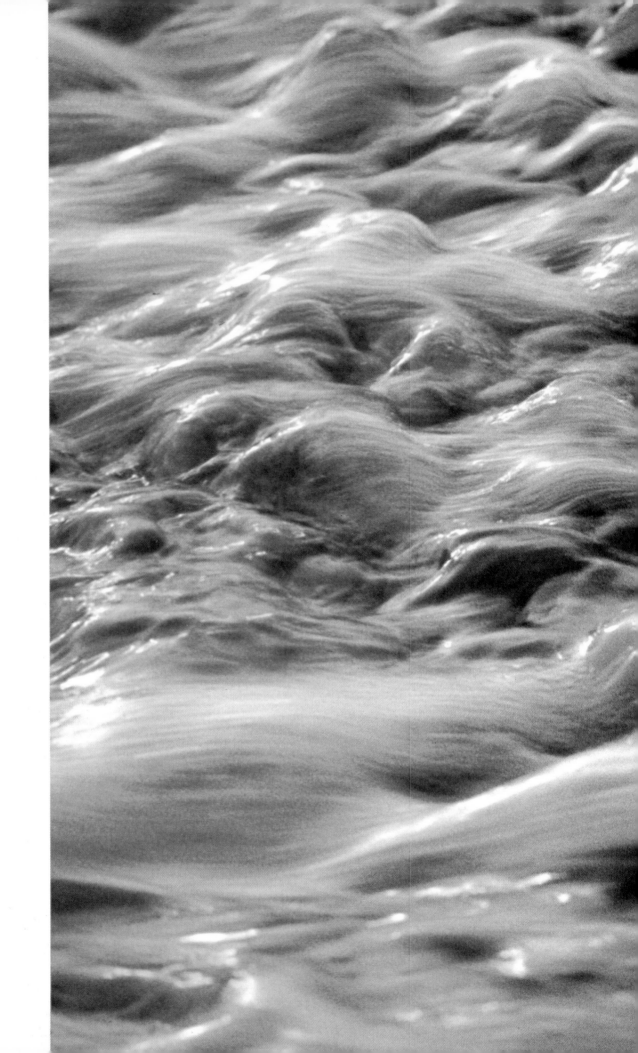

# ABOUT THE PICTURES

## by Ernest Braun

Sharing a discovery is one of a photographer's joys. Another, for me, is to encourage other people to look closer and to make their own discoveries. As little children we all start out with eyes close to the ground, seeing, feeling, smelling, exploring, and learning. Seeing with a camera is the best way I have found to get close to the earth again.

After looking at the pictures in this book, imagine that you are wandering with your camera along a wilderness trail, or that you are stretched out in a meadow at dawn, shivering with cold and delight as the rising sun gently prods the frost crystals. This scene will never be repeated. The elements, earth, air, fire, and water, are in a changing balance instant by instant. You see it change and raise your camera. This is a moment of confrontation. You are faced with infinite choices. What will you do? If both the environment and the camera are new to you, a quick snapshot may be enough; but if you have become aware of the endless possibilities for visual discovery, you will work longer and harder, though you will never be completely satisfied.

There is an entrancing subjective quality about nature photography. If you just open yourself to the environment and try to tune in on what is happening, you will begin to see images that almost reach out to be discovered. Pictures will seem to happen to you without any effort. But you will miss all this fun if you cling to rigid preconceived concepts of subject matter or a static way of seeing.

We all need a transition period between home or highway and the reality of the natural world. This is a time for walking, feeling the earth underfoot, visiting with the landscape, watching the light change and the clouds move, or maybe just listening to the many sounds of running water and wind in the trees. One of the best times I can remember was the beginning of a visit to Delaney Creek in Yosemite. I needed three days of solitude to unwind, to forget what day it was, to drop the load of personal problems. I had been up and down the stream, cameras and film in my daypack, walking for hours, sometimes sitting quietly on the rocky banks visually exploring the magic of water, until finally I was content to just be.

Although all my working life has been spent with a camera, I have been photographing in the natural world for a relatively short time—and never too seriously. My purpose has been, more than anything else, to learn and to be refreshed. But as I became better acquainted with nature and nature photography, I realized that the creative work of most contemporary photographers was confined to human experience. The rest of the planet was being neglected, and I knew that the visual arts could help by just showing how it is here before the asphalt and concrete take over. We cannot expect people to fight for something they don't even know.

I started camping and backpacking only ten years ago. Before that, I felt I was too busy with photographic assignments, being part of a family, expanding and remodeling an old house on a steep, forested hill. Then I began exploring nature in small ways—wandering on our hill with the children when they were small, exploring beaches and tidepools with them.

My first love was the tideline wilderness. During family vacations at the beach I began to explore its form, color, texture, and motion with a camera. As my work led me up and down the Pacific Coast, I managed a little extra time to explore and photograph other beaches, from San Diego to the Olympic Peninsula. So it was quite natural for me to carry a camera into the mountains.

As my friendship with the high country of the Sierra Nevada grew, my seeing with the camera became more intimate. I discovered that a great unknown exists at ground level. This is where the action is, in living and growing terms. I found, as I had in the tidepools, that when I stayed in one place, close to the ground with eyes and lens alert, my view of the world was transformed, and my opportunity for seeing and thinking was expanded. There was enough going on in one place for a whole day's work. Discovery was cut short only when a cloud of mosquitoes or a stiff neck forced me to my feet.

Because of the very limited time I had available and a general dissatisfaction with my random efforts, I decided to concentrate on a visual profile of a small area. By imposing this discipline on myself, I hoped that more intense exploration would be possible and that the feeling of intimacy I hoped to establish would be transferred through the pictures to the viewer. Three years ago, after a lot of looking, I selected a meadow, a stream, and a timberline lake that were easy to get to—the meadow is just four and a half driving hours from home—and planned to return to these places as often as possible through the seasons. It would be better, of course, to spend a whole year in one wilderness place, and I will someday. While I know my meadow and stream better with each visit, the time to complete this project has not been available. (And in honesty I must admit that I have not been disciplined enough to resist knapsack trips through other parts of the high country with my family and with friends.) However, one result of this experience is a growing collection of photographs from which the pictures in this book were selected.

Seeing, thinking, and feeling are the essential acts of photography. The camera is scarcely more important to a photographer than a typewriter is to a writer; however, photographers have a wider choice of tools than writers do, and there is no denying that the seeing and the tools are related. The traditional large-format view camera and the modern 35mm single-lens reflex camera represent the extremes. A wide range of camera systems lie in between and may be used in all kinds of ways. Each system has its advantages and its limitations. A contact print from an 8x10 negative can represent the ultimate in clarity and perfection. Because of the time, effort, and craftsmanship needed to operate a large view camera, each exposure is an important event that merits careful study and consideration. However, the photographer with his large camera on a tripod tends to be an observer rather than a participant. There is so much heavy equipment between him and his subject that his seeing becomes deliberate and limited. Portability is a problem, especially on long trail trips because pack animals are restricted to altitudes where grazing is available and allowed.

The compact 35mm single-lens reflex camera has many advantages for nature photography. One sees the same image through the lens that is being recorded on film. The mechanical barrier between the photographer and the environment is minimized. Since hardly any effort is needed to operate the camera, more energy is available for seeing. Most important, the camera is light, mobile, and easily used in tight spots. All this freedom must be used wisely. We live in a time of instant everything, and now instant images are here—thirty-six at a time, if one just keeps pushing the little button. The tiny 35mm format demands respect and loving care if the magnificent quality of modern lenses and film is not to be wasted by an unsteady hand or a careless eye.

As part of my preparation for teaching a photography workshop recently, I made a brief historical review of published nature photographs and was again reminded of the incredibly short and successful life of photography as a communication medium. Just one hundred years ago Sullivan and Jackson were recording Yosemite and the West for the first time. Their work is amazing, considering that there were no highways as we know them and they were using wet glass plates, coated and developed on the site in a tent darkroom carried on muleback. Minimum exposure time was fifteen seconds. About forty years ago Edward Weston was exploring the natural world with his 8x10 view camera. He discovered the texture, form, and symmetry that had always been there but had seldom been seen. In 1938 Kodachrome film became available and in the last ten years the single-lens reflex camera and faster color film arrived on the scene. I can't help wondering what Weston might have done with modern equipment!

While photographic technology has continued to make picture taking easier, serious photographers of the natural world have tended to be traditional in their seeing and thinking, feeling safer perhaps to work within the limitations of the large format camera. There has been almost a reverence for the needlesharp image, made popular by the *f*64 group. I think of this as a carryover from the early days of photography when a technically perfect image was a goal in itself. Actually, a totally sharp photograph is an abstraction. Our eyes scan as we look, never projecting a sharp image of the whole scene on the retina, but moving rapidly so that we have an impression of the whole. When we look intently at one point, nothing else is sharp.

My choice for wilderness photography is the 35mm camera. All the photographs in this book were made with Nikon or Pentax systems. Most of the pictures could not have been made with any other kind of equipment. I respect and use the view camera and the 2¼x2¼ format for some of my commercial work, but about 70 percent of my editorial, industrial, and advertising assignments are done with the 35mm. I seldom take a picture that gives me personal satisfaction with anything but the 35mm. This format gives me maximum freedom to identify with my subject.

I tend to be impatient with equipment and with myself because the image I see may not exist in another minute—the frost is melting, the bubbles under the ice are moving, and so are the clouds and the sun. There is an immediacy about closeup work that is exciting and demanding. You never know if the frog will jump before you are ready—and he usually does.

Except for a few telephoto shots and long exposures with neutral density filters, I do not use a tripod. A tripod takes time to set up and is extra weight to carry. Some good pictures are failures because of camera movement, but often there is a rock or a tree handy for extra support. It becomes a question of choosing your limitations.

The micro lenses are great time-savers for closeup work. They focus from infinity up to a point at which the image on the film is the same size as the subject. I also like the different perspective in a closeup image made with a longer focal length lens, such as the 200mm with added extension tubes. I use all the lenses that are available and moderately portable, from the 21mm focal length to the 500mm. If I am traveling very light, as on a long knapsack trip, I take one camera with the 55mm Micro-Nikkor and a 135mm lens. That is a minimum. If my back is up to it, I add a 28mm and the 200mm, plus another camera body.

Dawn and dusk are prime times for any kind of outdoor photography, because the light is soft and warm. Our sun has a tender goodbye caress for the land in the evening, while early morning is a time of cheerful reunion. As the light level diminishes, high speed color film extends the time for working, although I try to use slower fine-grain color film whenever possible. Cloudy or foggy days are ideal for closeups. Storms are a time of celebration for the land and present very special and beautiful conditions for working (it's surprising how wet a camera can get and still keep operating). The harsh light and strong shadows of the midday hours are very difficult, however, and the brightness range of a sunny day may exceed the capabilities of color film. The middle of the day is a good time to move on to the next campsite, to scout locations for work at dusk, or to enjoy a siesta after a dawn picture session.

# Photographic details

122 Sulphur butterfly (TOP) and monarch, Crane Flat Meadow, Yosemite. 200mm Nikkor lens plus extension tubes, High Speed Ektachrome.

123 Bumblebee visiting hound's tongue, Crane Flat Meadow, Yosemite. Micro-Nikkor lens, High Speed Ektachrome.

124 Grasshopper, Crane Flat Meadow, Yosemite. Micro-Nikkor lens, High Speed Ektachrome.

125 Mountain blue butterfly, Crane Flat Meadow, Yosemite. Micro-Nikkor lens, High Speed Ektachrome.

127 Dry grass spike, probably *Sitanion* sp., and golden rods, *Solidago* sp. Crane Flat Meadow, Yosemite. 200 mm Nikkor lens plus extension tubes, High Speed Ektachrome.

128 Dandelion seeds, Crane Flat Meadow, Yosemite. Micro-Nikkor lens, Ektachrome.

130 Through the growing season with the cow parsnip, *Heracleum lanatum*, in Crane Flat Meadow, Yosemite. Buds and flowers with 135mm Nikkor lens, seed with Micro-Nikkor lens; High Speed Ektachrome.

131 Cow parsnip seed; same as page 130.

134 Yellow staghorn lichen, *Letharia vulpina*, extremely abundant throughout the fir forest on the mid-slopes of the Sierra, harbors the residence of a spider here at the edge of Crane Flat Meadow, Yosemite. 500mm Aetna Coligon lens with tripod.

135 Beneath a neighboring Jeffrey pine, *Pinus jeffreyi*, old cones lie beside lupines and bracken ferns. 85mm Nikkor lens. High Speed Ektachrome.

137 The dominant tree in the mid-slope Sierran climax forest is the red fir, *Abies magnifica*, here photographed on the slopes above Yosemite Creek, about 8,000 ft. elevation. 85mm Nikkor lens, High Speed Ektachrome.

140 Autumn frost just melted by the morning sun, hanging in drops from the seed spikes of a delicate grass, Crane Flat Meadow, Yosemite. Micro-Nikkor lens, High Speed Ektachrome.

141 TOP: Morning mist rising from Crane Flat Meadow, Yosemite. Lodgepole pines, *Pinus contorta* var. *murrayana*, line the edge of the meadow. 135mm Nikkor lens, High Speed Ektachrome. BOTTOM: Cumulus clouds at sunset, airplane view. 135mm Nikkor lens, High Speed Ektachrome.

144 Edge of Crane Flat Meadow, Yosemite. 135mm Nikkor lens, Kodachrome II.

146 Merced River Canyon, foothills below Yosemite Valley. 135mm Nikkor lens, Ektachrome-X. Ponderosa pine, *Pinus ponderosa*; Douglas fir, *Pseudotsuga taxifolia*; and Maul or canyon live oak, *Quercus chrysolepis*, are especially abundant trees on the slopes of foothill canyons.

147 Alder trees, *Alnus* sp., braving the rapids of spring thaw in Wildcat Creek, Yosemite. 135mm Nikkor lens, High Speed Ektachrome.

150 California poppies, *Eschscholtzia californica*, from a steep slope in the Merced River Canyon, foothills below Yosemite. 135mm lens, High Speed Ektachrome.

151 Dry grass; same as page 150.

153 Alluvium, Merced River below Yosemite, in summer. 135mm Nikkor lens, Ektachrome-X.

154 Thistle parachutes among cattail leaves, at Ruth Lake, Los Banos Wildlife Area, Merced County. Micro-Nikkor lens, Ektachrome-X.

155 Tricolored blackbirds, *Agelaius tricolor*; same as page 154.

156 Stanislaus River west of Modesto, San Joaquin Valley. Micro-Nikkor lens, Ektachrome-X.

157 Same as page 156.

158 Detail of feather in the river-bank jungle, Caswell Memorial Park, on the Stanislaus River west of Modesto. Micro-Nikkor lens, Ektachrome-X.

159 Shoot of wild grape, *Vitis californica*, photographed against the canopy of trees overhead. 135mm Nikkor lens, Ektachrome-X.

160 Cracked mud, Button-Willow Lake, Los Banos Wildlife Area, Merced County. Micro-Nikkor lens, High Speed Ektachrome.

162 Short-billed dowitchers, *Limnodromus griseus*, feeding in a pickleweed marsh on a foggy morning; Lower Tubbs Island, San Pablo Bay, Sonoma County. 500mm lens, High Speed Ektachrome.

163 Pickleweed detail, *Salicornia* sp., photographed against a pattern of cracks in the muddy bottom, Lower Tubbs Island. 135mm Nikkor lens, High Speed Ektachrome.

167 Sunset over the Lower Tubbs Island marshes, San Pablo Bay, Sonoma County, viewed through wild summer mustards gone to seed. 24mm lens, Ektachrome-X.

170 Beach grass, *Ammophila arenaria*, holding the dunes at Drake's Bay, Marin County. 28mm Schneider lens, High Speed Ektachrome.

171 Feather and bubbles among eel grass scraps washed ashore in a winter storm, Drake's Bay, Marin County. Macro-Kilar lens, High Speed Ektachrome.

175 Tide-washed pebbles at Point Lobos; 1/2 second exposure at dusk, with camera resting on a beach rock. Macro-Kilar lens, Kodachrome II.

# Index

Body type, 12-point Spectrum; display faces, Centaur and Arrighi. Composition by Mackenzie & Harris, Inc., San Francisco. Printed by Graphic Arts Center, Portland. Design by David Cavagnaro, Ernest Braun, and Raymond Andersen.